ALCOHOLISM:
Time and Recovery

ALCOHOLISM:
Time and Recovery

A series of twelve talks by Donald L. Carriere, M.S.,
alcoholism therapist and member of the Michigan
Association of Alcoholism and Drug Abuse Counselors
and the National Association of Alcoholism Counselors.

Compiled and edited by Muriel Doehr-Hadcock, B.G.S.

VANTAGE PRESS
New York

FIRST EDITION

Copyright © 1991 by Muriel L. Hadcock

Published by Vantage Press, Inc.
516 West 34th Street, New York, New York 10001

Manufactured in the United States of America
ISBN: 0-533-08927-1

Library of Congress Catalog Card No.: 89-90577
1 2 3 4 5 6 7 8 9 0

To Randy, Jay, Jody, Loren,
Deb, Ruth, Rob, Kent, and Irene

Contents

Acknowledgments

These talks on alcoholism are a result of several years of involvement with the alcoholism therapy department of a suburban hospital.

To Washtenaw Community College, Ypsilanti, Michigan, my thanks for an excellent training in substance abuse therapy are further extended.

The authors wish to thank Albert Ellis, Ph.D., for permission to use excerpts from the book titled *A New Guide to Rational Living*.

The authors extend appreciation to Lorraine Meier and Kristine Blahnik of Wayne State University for their assistance in proofreading and editing the text, to Joan Snider for typing and working out those final touches before publication of the original manuscript, and to Bill Radak for his assistance and encouragement.

To the alcoholics and problem drinkers who have listened to my talks, asked questions, and explored my logic many thanks and keep going on the road to recovery.

To the people in the Detroit metropolitan area who are active in helping other people recover from alcohol abuse or alcoholism I wish to express my thanks and admiration for your dedication to the solution of a most difficult problem.

Finally, thanks to my good buddy Pete, who was a terrible drinker, a man with many years of bad drinking experiences, a man who lost his wife through death from alcohol, a man whose children are permanently scarred by his drinking, but a man who in the last seven years of his life realized that he was an alcoholic, gave up alcohol, and worked at recovery, a man whom I met in the hospital and watched turn from a drunken Tennessee hillbilly to a fine southern gentleman, and a man who unfortunately died of a heart attack due to heart damage incurred during his drinking years, but a man who died with pride and dignity and with the knowledge that he was successful in recovery.

As a tribute to Pete, some of us who worked with him in his recovery from alcoholism erected a plaque in a hospital meeting room where Pete had attended many alcoholism therapy sessions. This plaque contains a message that was composed by Tom G., another recovering alcoholic. It says that Pete was one among many people attempting to recover from alcoholism but that Pete was successful in that he was "ONE AMONG FEW" who actually did something about his alcoholism by working at recovery. Thanks, Pete, for helping me understand alcoholism.

Introduction

The reader will find that this book is actually a collection of a series of twelve talks on the subject of alcohol, rather than a written narrative. These are typical talks, as presented to groups of twenty or sixty people, and they are usually accompanied by diagrams that had been drawn in chalk on a blackboard. As closely as possible, the talks are unedited to retain an "off-the-cuff" flavor of speaking. As a result, some literary accuracy or coherence may have been sacrificed. Keep in mind that the book is not intended for scholars but was written to help the alcohol abuser. Most of the modern day alcohol treatment programs in hospitals, et cetera, have a similar series of talks (didactics), which are presented both to in-patients and out-patients. In fact, much of the material for this book has been gleaned from listening to many speakers on the subject of alcohol abuse.

The book is arranged to give the reader, first of all, an idea of what kind of drug alcohol is, what physical damage results from the abuse of alcohol, how people learn to drink, and what distinguishes the alcoholic and problem drinker from other people who drink alcohol. The middle of the book contains the heart of the talks, titled "Time and Recovery," which is a procedure to arrest a drinking problem. The remainder of the book contains information on aids helpful in recovery, including a final talk which summarizes the complete book.

If you enjoy drinking alcohol and are not currently experiencing any alcohol-related problems, this book may be of general interest to you. If you are one of the estimated forty percent of adult Americans who have a problem with alcohol, you might be mildly interested in this book. However, if you are one of the ten percent of adult Americans suffering from the disease alcoholism, this book may help save your life. In other words, the success of this book in helping people with an alcohol problem depends on the motivation of the reader. Unfortunately, one of the most serious problems in helping problem drinkers, alcohol abusers, or alcoholics is a lack of motivation by the person with the problem. Therefore, it is suggested that the reader keep an open mind, read the book completely, and then decide if he is sufficiently motivated to start a recovery program of his own.

Unfortunately, no questions may be solicited from the audience. However, the talks are built primarily from audience queries during talks which were given over the past few years.

If you are sincere in wanting to do something about a drinking problem or the disease alcoholism, for yourself or some other person, you should find the book very helpful.

ALCOHOLISM:
Time and Recovery

Talk 1

Mood-altering Drugs*

*A figure typical of that used for a blackboard presentation is included with most of the talks as a visual aid. These figures are also included for use by other therapists presenting this material.

HALLUCINOGENS	STIMULANTS	OPIATES	SEDATIVES
"MIND EXPANDERS"	"UPPERS"	"DREAMERS"	"DOWNERS" (anxiety)
LSD	NICOTINE	OPIUM	VALIUM
PCP	CAFFEINE	MORPHINE	LIBRIUM
MESCALINE	DEXEDRINE	HEROIN	MELLARIL
PEYOTE	BENZEDRINE	METHADONE	SERAX
MARIJUANA	AMPHETAMINES	DEMEROL	THORAZINE
"WHY	(speed freaks)	PERCODAN	BARBITURATES
DO	COCAINE	LOMOTH	SECONAL
WE		CODEINE	NEMBUTAL
DRUG			PHENOBARBITAL
OURSELVES?"			QUAALUDES
			CHLORAL HYDRATE
			ALCOHOL
NON-ADDICTIVE	ADDICTIVE	HIGHLY ADDICTIVE	VERY ADDICTIVE
SECONDARY KILLER	SECONDARY KILLER	SECONDARY KILLER	"KILLER"

To begin our talks, I will attempt to make you aware of how alcohol fits in with other drugs and show you how the drug alcohol is classified. Some people can relate to this better if we show them other commonly used mood-altering drugs. We will concentrate on the abuse aspect of using these drugs, rather than on some of the good things that you get from them. There are four major mood-altering drug categories:

- HALLUCINOGENS
- STIMULANTS
- OPIATES
- SEDATIVES

HALLUCINOGENS

If you're much over forty years of age then you probably haven't dealt much with hallucinogens, but stimulants, opiates, and sedatives might have touched your life. If you're forty years or younger, you might have tried hallucinogens. This is primarily because hallucinogens, although they're been around for years, became popular in this country during the sixties. Hallucinogens are primarily mind expanders. The way they work is that they take your thoughts, your normal thoughts, and somehow expand those thoughts in your brain. It's similar to the way you sometimes take an idle thought and expand it way out of proportion. For instance, if I saw a person sitting here with a red shirt on while I was under the effects of a strong hallucinogen, I might associate that color red in my mind with fire. Expanding this thought in my mind, I might think, *If that's fire, that person must be on fire,* and I might rush over to beat out the flames. In so doing, I might injure that person or he may injure me because he thinks I'm crazy.

One of the common hallucinogens, perhaps the strongest of all, is LSD. It was very popular in this country in the 1960s. Originally LSD was used as a psychiatric-type drug to help chronically withdrawn people. These people had trouble developing thoughts in their minds and ex-

3

pressing them. Psychiatry was looking for a drug to help these people open up by making their minds more fluid in order to enable them to express their thoughts and, consequently, develop a more meaningful personality. Fortunately, the drug does work very well that way. Unfortunately, some people use it as a party drug on which they can take trips. While in a drugged state and hallucinating, some people get into serious trouble. One of the most common occurrences while under the effects of hallucinogens is looking out a window and getting the idea that you can fly like a bird. This is all right if you're on the first floor, because you can dive out that window and find out you can't fly. But if you're on the third floor, there's a good chance you'll kill yourself. We know this is true because some people have recovered from these falls and been able to describe the experience. They actually thought they were birds. One of the most publicized cases is the daughter of a well-known television personality. His daughter died after a fall from an upper floor window. She suffered an LSD flashback experience, and it's suspected that she tried to fly, resulting in a fall and death.

We don't see too much LSD now, but we do see a great deal of what is called angel dust or hog—PCP. It's plentiful because it's easily manufactured. You can manufacture about a quarter of a million dollars' worth (street value) of PCP for around two thousand dollars. The drug is used primarily as a street drug by teenagers or even subteenagers and used at the junior high school level. It's pushed on these young people because the manufacturers are trying to make money. Originally, it was an animal tranquillizer, but it works as a hallucinogen on humans.

In its abuse, the main problem with PCP is that like all other drugs, it has to be broken down in the body and this particular drug is very difficult for the body to break down. One of the dangers is that the user will continue to hallucinate as long as the drug is in the body, and this happens frequently to children who take an abnormal quantity of the drug. They begin to hallucinate, and the hallucinations won't stop. The children become panic-stricken and usually end up in the emergency room of the hospital. It's sad, but there is really nothing the doctor can do for them except wait for the drug to be broken down in the body. Children's Hospital in the Detroit area has done a great deal of research in an attempt to find ways to speed up the process of breaking down PCP in the body. In some cases, the temporary panic-stricken state leads to an almost permanent psychosis, i.e., a permanent mental breakdown. The users are so fear-stricken that it causes their minds to want to withdraw. Even when the effect of the drug has worn off, the withdrawn state still exists. It's

4

hard to overcome this problem once it develops, so PCP is really a very dangerous drug. But it's also a common, very common, drug.

Some other hallucinogens we see are mescaline and peyote. These are older-type drugs used as ceremonial drugs for many years by the Indian people in the Southwest United States. Some of these drugs found their way onto the street in the fifties and sixties. They are not overly strong hallucinogens, so they don't present a danger to most people.

A common drug people think they can buy is THC or T, which is the principal active ingredient in marijuana. It is the ingredient in marijuana that gives people the drugged effect. It's very hard to extract from the marijuana plant, so you aren't really buying so-called T on the street. About the only place it's synthesized in this country is a federal government laboratory in Mississippi where it's extracted for experimental purposes. So if you think you're buying T on the street, you're probably buying PCP or LSD laced with milk sugar, strychnine, rat poisoning, or something like that. The reason I bring this up is because of a technicality. Since THC is the active ingredient in marijuana and since it's a hallucinogen, technically we would classify marijuana as a hallucinogen. However, it can act as a stimulant or a sedative. Usually, it's a hallucinogen and the hallucinogenic effect is what people are looking for. Marijuana can be a panic drug because one of its effects is to elevate the pulse. When people become aware of this rapid pulse, panic sets in. By rapid pulse I mean that a pulse of 80 beats per minute becomes elevated to 120 beats per minute. That's very noticeable in your body and can panic you. Other derivatives of the marijuana plant, such as hashish or similar drugs, have stronger concentrations of THC. The effects, though, are about the same.

Not dwelling too much longer on hallucinogens, there are a couple more things we can say about them. First, they aren't what we call addictive. In other words, it's very difficult, if not rare, for people to become addicted to hallucinogens. I will talk more about addiction with some of the other drugs, but what the lack of addictive qualities means here is that users can stop taking hallucinogens without any apparent difficulty. They don't develop any serious symptoms when they're away from the drug, even if they've been using it over a period of time. Second, we don't consider hallucinogens too much of a health hazard, although they can cause some minor health problems. As for the effect on the lungs, there is some evidence to indicate that one marijuana cigarette may be the equivalent of twenty normal nicotine cigarettes. But school's really out on the effects of the use of the hallucinogens—marijuana in particular. Research is being done, but nothing has been definitely proven. One thing we know is that there aren't many deaths due to the use of these drugs. Maybe people on the drugs do something that can kill them, but technically the drugs are not the killers.

The strongest argument against the use of hallucinogens is probably a philosophical one: What is there about our society that causes people to want to go around in a drugged state? This particular argument will probably prevent the legalization of marijuana, because our society has difficulty addressing this issue.

STIMULANTS

Stimulants are another drug category. We think of stimulants as being "uppers." If you're dragged out and tired, either physically, mentally, or both, the effect of a stimulant is to give you a lift.

One of the most common stimulants is nicotine. I mention this one first because it's the reason people smoke cigarettes. I'll explain this a little with an example. In England, nine or ten years ago a cigarette was marketed which was nicotine-free. As far as the smoking regimen, it had all the flavor and satisfaction of a regular nicotine cigarette, but it had no nicotine in it. When the cigarettes first came out, they sold like hotcakes. For about a week, people were really snapping them up. But after that first week sales began to fall off, and by the third week the stores couldn't even give the things away. People would smoke them but say, "This is fine, but something's missing." Well, we know what was missing—it was the nicotine. Now we're beginning to get the idea a little bit about addiction.

You've probably heard someone say, "I'm not addicted to cigarettes; I can easily give them up—I've quit a hundred times." Well, this means they can give them up, but they will always go back to them. The reason they go back is that they've developed a need for cigarettes. Any of you who have been heavy smokers and tried to quit usually find that the first day is not too bad. You begin to think a little bit about cigarettes, and you're a little nervous. On the second day, though, some very dramatic symptoms begin to occur. An inordinate craving for cigarettes develops,

6

and you begin to notice who is smoking and who isn't; also, there are a few changes in your body. You may develop sweaty palms or feel a little headachy, or your stomach may begin growling. By the third day, these symptoms intensify. You may feel like you've a mild case of the flu, because these are the body's reactions to withdrawal from nicotine. By the fourth day these symptoms begin to subside gradually, and by the seventh day you feel pretty good. Physiologically, you've withdrawn from nicotine and your body doesn't really crave it anymore. However, you've got a hell of a battle ahead of you. You'll find that for the next year you will crave a cigarette whenever you're in a situation where you once used cigarettes. That's a psychological need you've developed, and it's really the psychological need or dependence on cigarettes that's the most difficult to break. So now you're getting the idea of what addiction is all about.

Addiction Is Need—
It Can Be Mental, Physical, or Both

Stimulants, as I said before, stimulate you physiologically. If you're a cigarette smoker, one way to get a handle on this stimulation is to take your pulse while smoking a cigarette. It will be around 95 or higher. Take your pulse again half an hour or forty-five minutes after you've stopped smoking the cigarette; you'll find your pulse has dropped from 10 to 20 beats per minute. This is due to the stimulating effect of nicotine.

Coffee also has a stimulating effect. I think we're all pretty aware of the presence of caffeine in coffee and its stimulating effect. Some folks can't get going in the morning without a couple cups of coffee. Waking in the morning, they'll say, "I'm so slow and groggy. I'd better have a cup of coffee." A couple cups of coffee seem to wake them up a little so they're ready for the day. Some people drink it all day to keep going and can't sleep at night. They may even wonder what's wrong with them because they can't sleep. Well, what's wrong is they've abused caffeine—they've not used it properly.

Caffeine also has the property of suppressing your appetite. All stimulants seem to have this particular property. As we get into stronger stimulants, one of the most common ones would be Dexedrine, which became a popular appetite depressant. It was prescribed by doctors as a reducing aid, but many people abused the drug. They seemed to think that if the doctor said, "Take one or two," perhaps four or five would work even better. As a consequence, we ended up with many nervous people walking around. The abuse of Dexedrine became epidemic in this country. Housewives exchanged pills with their neighbors, and prescriptions were forged. In trying to use it as a weight reducer, people actually developed very nervous dispositions and became very uncomfortable. The situation was out of control and became so serious that the Food and Drug Administration clamped down on Dexedrine. First, they limited prescriptions to six months so you had to return to your doctor every six months to get a new prescription. In a further attempt to control the drug, the Food and Drug people finally changed the classification of Dexedrine from a readily available drug to one with severe restrictions. It is now necessary for the druggist to keep Dexedrine with narcotics in a safe. So you see what can happen with a popular prescription drug.

Also interesting about Dexedrine is that non-prescription, over-the-counter reducing aids rather than being amphetamines (like Dexedrine) are really large amounts of caffeine and a decongestant.

By a large amount, I mean that one tablet or capsule contains as much caffeine as two or three cups of coffee. This is combined with a decongestant, the same as in a pill to relieve nasal congestion. The decongestant is put in to aid people in getting rid of water from the body, as an indication of weight loss. Here we have a milder stimulant, caffeine, replacing a strong drug, while the manufacturers attempted to cash in on the publicity given Dexedrine as a reducing aid by changing the name slightly.

Another kind of stimulant that people use is Benzedrine. Benzedrine is one of the original amphetamines. At one time in this country, you could buy what was called a Benzedrine inhaler. If you had a stuffy nose, you'd sniff on the Benzedrine inhaler and you could breathe normally again, because one of the properties of stimulants is causing your nasal membranes to shrink. This inhaler was a plastic tube with a paper packing which had been dipped in a solution of Benzedrine and aromatics. People soon realized that this particular inhaler contained Benzedrine, and rather than sticking it in their nose, they would remove the wicking, stick it in a bottle of Coke or beer, and wait for the Benzedrine to go into the solution. Drinking the contents would give them a sufficient amount of Benzedrine to keep them awake for about three days. A normally quiet person would become very excitable and start talking and might even become a nonstop talker for about three days. Of course, you become very tired after about a day of no sleep, and you may lie down, but your pulse is elevated, your respiration is elevated, and your mind is going around and around so you can't sleep. After about three days you begin to get bug-eyed, actually bug-eyed, because the pressure behind your eyeballs has built up. You're very fatigued and agitated mentally and become a very ornery person. This drugged effect is very difficult to handle but wears off in about three days. If no one has hassled you, you'll sleep for a day or two and come out of it feeling pretty good.

The abuse of this inhaler became so bad that the Food and Drug Administration had to take it off the market, too. People became wise to the fact that it had Benzedrine in it. One place it was abused was in our prisons. While visiting your brother-in-law in prison you could give him two dozen Benzedrine inhalers for his nasal condition. There was nothing in the law which said you couldn't do this. So Benzedrine inhalers came off the market, too, and now inhalers do not contain Benzedrine. Another form of Benzedrine is known by the common slang name *Benny.* Bennys were used by our Armed Forces during World War II—particularly by people in combat to keep them awake on missions.

Although Benzedrine can be called one of the original amphetamines, a whole school of amphetamines with various prefixes, such as *meth, dextro,* et cetera, has been developed. Unfortunately, in the sixties we developed drug abusers who became addicted to the amphetamines. They were tagged with the name *speed freaks.* Speed freaks are usually white males in their twenties or early thirties, and they're usually scrawny guys because they don't eat right. The stimulant they're using kills their appetite, and they're also highly agitated. Inner-city people or blacks seldom use amphetamines, but many white, suburban youths use speed. In their need for it, many of them turn to petty thievery, so they also have legal problems. Unfortunately, most hospitals don't want anything to do with speed freaks because they're so difficult to control. Being so agitated, they won't sit down or lie down, and hospitals hate to forcefully restrain anybody. Speed freaks experience wide mood swings and become antagonistic and violent. Consequently, most hospitals advise people who bring them in to take them home and talk them down. Their youth usually protects them from any physical medical difficulties. Of course, if they were older and abusing stimulants, they might develop heart or blood pressure problems and require hospital care. There is one danger about which most hospitals advise people coming off amphetamines. When they go home, they have to be very careful because they can become

9

extremely suicide-prone when coming off the drug. There's a reason for this. If we drug ourselves from a norm to a highly stimulated state, we don't come back to the norm when the drug wears off. Our bodies are programmed so that we overshoot the mark and go into a depressed state. It also seems that human beings are programmed in such a way that depression leads to thoughts of suicide, and the deeper that depression the greater the chances of actually committing suicide. This is really the greatest danger of amphetamine abuse.

One drug I haven't mentioned which belongs with the stimulants is cocaine (also called snow, crack or nose candy). Cocaine is a stimulant originally used by the Indians of South America. It wasn't a very strong drug, because they would chew the leaves of the coca plant, thus extracting the cocaine. However, in the refined state, as used by drug abusers, cocaine has a peculiar property. It has the properties of the other stimulants but also develops a fairly strong psychological addiction. There has been a rise in the popularity of cocaine in the form of crack in this country because many young people think that cocaine is an aphrodisiac or sexual stimulant. Rightly or wrongly, that's what leads to some of its popularity. Cocaine derivatives give you a pleasant high, and one dose may last a half hour, then wear off. Some people begin to like the feeling so they go back for more, thereby developing an exceptionally strong psychological dependence on cocaine. Also, some researchers claim that cocaine and its derivatives are physically addictive. Except for the opiates, cocaine is the only drug in this country which comes under the jurisdiction of the federal narcotics laws. The reason for this is not because it's as dangerous as most substance abuse therapists perceive the opiates to be, but when the Harrison Act was put together in the early 1900s, rightly or wrongly, some people claim that southern legislators in this country blamed many of their problems on the black people in the South and their use of cocaine. Therefore, they filibustered to retain cocaine under the federal narcotics laws. For most people, it's really not a dangerous drug when compared to the opiates, but it's still classified with opiates. Generally, for our population, these stimulants aren't physical killers; however, news headlines, as everyone knows, reveal sudden deaths of people abusing stimulants. As another example, malnutrition due to poor eating habits because you don't have an appetite can result in some abuse to the body, and there is a tendency toward being suicide-prone. These effects, considering our population as a whole, are secondary, and we can call stimulants secondary killers. However, stimulants are both mildly psychologically and physiologically addictive if abused and tolerance build-up leads to increasingly larger doses to achieve the same effect.

OPIATES

Opiates are our next drug category. Opiates are dreamers. Their effect? They'll put you in a very dreamy state. They're also what we call narcotics. All drugs aren't narcotics. The opiates, with the exception of cocaine, are what we call narcotics and are classified under the federal narcotics laws. The original opiate, which comes from the opium poppy flower, of course is opium. The principal derivative from opium is morphine, and the value of morphine is that it's an analgesic—it's a painkiller. The medical use of opiates is really the only valid use for them. The reason they've been around for so many years is they're terrific painkillers, both psychologically and physiologically. Let's start by understanding the painkiller morphine. Here is an example of the dreamy state it puts you in. Normally, if I walked up to you with a knife and said, "I'm going to cut your finger off," you'd have a "hemorrhage," so to speak. You wouldn't want me to cut your finger off. However, if I injected you with an amount of morphine sufficient to put you in a dreamy state (but not sleep), I could probably walk up to you with a knife and say, "I'm going to cut your finger off," and you wouldn't protest at all. You'd be willing to sit there and watch me cut your finger off. In fact, I could probably tell you that I was going to cut your head off and you wouldn't protest. There are a couple of reasons for that. First, you won't feel any pain when I put that knife to your finger, because morphine is a physical painkiller. Second, you don't want any psychological pain. To protest or hassle me, to say, "I don't want you to cut off my finger" is psychological pain, which you can't feel in the drugged state. You don't want that, so you wouldn't risk getting in an argument with me. That feeling, that dreamy state, is described as perhaps the most pleasant of human experiences . . . a dreamy, drift-through-life state, with no psychological or physical pain whatsoever. You're not capable of feeling any true human feelings or emotions, but you experience a wonderful escape feeling. Once you develop an addiction to that feeling you're in trouble, because outside of using opiates you'll have a problem ever recapturing that feeling naturally or by using drugs other than opiates.

Now, as in the case of morphine, there are many derivatives of opium, including the common street drug heroin. Heroin is a combination of natural and synthetic opiates, a chemically developed drug. Years ago, the dregs of the opium poppy were thrown away after the morphine had been extracted because it was considered junk, i.e., garbage, hence the name *junkie*. Chemists found that by chemically treating this junk they could develop the drug heroin. A dose of heroin can have five to ten times the effect of an equivalent dose of morphine, so it's a very strong drug. People develop an addiction to heroin (also morphine), and it is a common street drug. So if you're looking for that dreamy state, heroin may be the only thing that'll give it to you. (The effect of heroin depends on the make-up of the user.) But heroin is an interesting drug; we read about it in the paper quite often. When people who are addicted to heroin attempt to withdraw from it (after prolonged use), they develop many of the same symptoms as people withdrawing from nicotine. However, we would have to magnify these symptoms by one hundred or one thousand. A person withdrawing from heroin generally feels like he has the world's worst case of flu. His mind wanders. Fluid is coming from every orifice in his body. His stomach is sick and he's having muscle spasms, among other things. He's really a thoroughly miserable creature. The only relief from these symptoms is another opiate or time. However, the thing that we find about withdrawing from heroin or any of the opiates is that people get awfully ill, but nobody dies. Most people who work with heroin addicts have never seen a death caused by withdrawing from heroin. Any deaths are due to secondary problems.

In World War II, the Germans had difficulty obtaining morphine, so they developed synthetics. One of these which we hear about is methadone. Another one is Demerol and there are many others. I have mentioned these two because they are most common. In most hospitals, Demerol is used as a painkiller instead of morphine. Methadone is also a painkiller, but it isn't as strong an analgesic as Demerol. It's effective in curbing psychological pain. Heroin addicts are very difficult to treat. In fact, some people claim that it's impossible to control heroin addiction, and studies seem to agree with this. One of the largest studies done (by the federal government) of people discharged from the U.S. Public Health Service Hospital in Lexington, Kentucky, surveyed one hundred people over a thirteen-year period to see what happened to them after they were released. There were a couple of deaths, but of the ninety-eight people every one of them had returned to heroin—not only once but several times. Many of these people had to be re-admitted for treatment. Some people believe the only way to control that addiction is to put the addicts on another drug, and that drug, of course, is methadone. That's why we read about methadone. It will satisfy that psychological craving and get rid of withdrawal symptoms and allow the addict to live an almost normal life. It doesn't match the dreamy state of heroin, and if heroin is taken while someone is on methadone, methadone has the property of diminishing the effects of heroin. This is why many heroin addicts don't like the methadone treatment.

Demerol is a painkiller used in some hospitals which don't have a federal license to help people withdraw from heroin with methadone. Withdrawal from heroin is extremely painful. As an example, a fellow about thirty-two years old had been admitted for heroin addiction and the doctor was withdrawing him from heroin by using Demerol. In the same room was an older fellow who was dying from cancer of the prostate. The doctors were giving the fellow withdrawing from heroin twice the dosage of Demerol as the fellow dying with cancer. The man with cancer died, but the former addict got out after spending about ten weeks in the hospital. They cut him back enough so that he was able to function quite well on low amounts of Demerol. I haven't seen him in two or three years, but I'm willing to bet that he's back on heroin now.

You can become innocently involved in this opiate problem. It was reported, as an example, that an outstanding Hollywood comedian's doctor prescribed Percadon for him. Percadon contains a synthetic opiate and two or three other little drugs—it's a very good painkiller. Evidently, this man had hurt his back and the doctor prescribed Percadon. However, he became addicted to it. He's still addicted and has publicly discussed his addiction. The opiates are highly addictive drugs; we like that "no pain" state. Imagine the simplest pain, such as stubbing your toe or finger, and not feeling it. However, if you're addicted to heroin but off it, your pain sensations are not controlled and the pain will be excruciating. You won't be able to handle it, and you'll want the drug. As I talk to young people I tell them, "If you're going to mess around with drugs, don't mess around with heroin, because it's tantamount to a death sentence. It may not kill you, but your ability to function as a human being is almost permanently lost." Young men have come to me after this talk and said that I hit it right on the head. They're heroin addicts, and they're having one hell of a time. It's a terrible circumstances to be in. However, if you use opiates enough to control yourself, there isn't much damage to the body. In fact, autopsies performed on medical people, in particular doctors in their eighties who had a long-standing addiction to morphine (fifty to sixty years) haven't shown any abnormal organ damage. So technically the opiates are not killers, only secondary killers. Surprisingly, it's very difficult and in some cases impossible to overdose on opiates. What will happen is that the functions of the addict will slow down to the point where he'll die. Casual use of opiates doesn't lead to death, and many so-called heroin overdose deaths are not due to heroin—they're due to combining heroin with another drug. We'll take that subject up shortly.

SEDATIVES

Sedatives are the drugs that predominate in this country. Sedatives are downers. If you're all worked up about something, a sedative will slow you down. I repeat: downers. Their most common use is to control a neurosis called anxiety, because we're very anxiety-ridden in this country. We fight and squabble among ourselves, and we have many problems. We resent authority, even shoot our presidents. We're highly competitive people. Although there aren't many of us who are psychotic or insane, we often use the expression "So-and-so must be nuts." Surprisingly, though, very rarely will we ever meet anybody who is insane. If you don't believe me, you should visit a state mental hospital to see some of the people who are truly psychotic. Then you can get an idea of what an insane person is. On the other hand, you won't meet anyone whose life is so well rounded that he has no problems whatsoever and lives in a complete state of bliss. We're all somewhere in the middle, suffering from some everyday neuroses. The one that predominates is anxiety. So what do we do? Go to the doctor and tell him, "Doc, I'm so damned nervous I don't know what the hell to do." The doctor says, "Well, wait a minute. I can take care of that for you. I'll prescribe something. Go home and take one of these every three hours." He prescribes something like Valium or Librium, so you have the prescription filled, take one, and wait. Hell, nothing happens. You're still upset, so after three hours you take another one. You seem to be functioning all right but still feel nervous and jittery. So you say to yourself, *Maybe the doctor was in a hurry and meant three every hour instead of one every three hours.* So you try that and that seems to work a little better. But then again, doctors are always a bit conservative because they don't want to overprescribe drugs, so you tell yourself, *I could probably take six every hour.* That's what some people do. You can see these people walking around, and if you were to ask them how they felt, they'd reply, "Great. I don't have any nervous problems anymore." However, they look like zombies because they're stoned on tranquillizers. These are so-called minor tranquillizers, but they are heavily prescribed. Valium holds first place in doctor-prescribed drugs, and Librium is third in the United States.

The way tranquillizers work is by affecting your power of concentration. If you looked at me, you might say, "Gee, that guy has on a silly-looking tie." This thought keeps going around in your mind until you say, "He not only has a silly-looking tie, but his face is silly, too." You just keep mulling it over until you're in such a state that you may want to come up here and punch me in the nose. We become very agitated and build mountains out of molehills. Thoughts are blown out of proportion.

On tranquilizers, however, you may experience the opposite effect. You may look at this tie and think, *That's a silly tie,* and begin to think about it but find you can't concentrate on it. You mind is wandering to something else. Your power of concentration is blocked. Some people even have difficulty reading a book when they're on tranquillizers. When they're on page two, they can't remember what they read back on page one because they can't concentrate. These are stronger tranquillizers, such as Serax, Mellaril, Thorazine, and many others.

These tranquillizers came on the market in the mid-fifties, and sales are still going strong. The situation is bad, not just because these drugs are so popular in the street, but because they're so readily available. The situation is similar to the abuse of Dexedrine. The Food and Drug Administration has already put the renewal time for some tranquillizer prescriptions at six months, but if the abuse continues, they'll come off the market, too. The companies which produce these drugs are making millions of dollars, so it's to be expected that they'll lobby like hell to keep them on the market. The federal government is trying to stop the medical profession from overprescribing tranquillizers, and some physicians are reacting by not prescribing them anymore. You don't need tranquillizers; there are non-chemical ways of coping. We've become a chemical-dependent society, and we don't need tranquillizers except in an extreme medical emergency.

15

Some drugs work pretty well during the day, but at night sleep becomes a problem. The doc says, "Well, I'll take care of that. We'll give you some Seconal at night or Nembutal. You just take these at night before you go to bed, and you'll sleep." You take the sleep drug, and it really works. The doc's right. In fact, you say, "This works better than the medicine the doctor gave me to take during the day. It works so well I'll take this during the day, too." People do that—take sleeping pills during the day. These are barbiturates and there are many of them, too. We have sub-categories of barbiturates: fast-acting and slow-acting. The fast-acting barbiturates are the dangerous ones. Slow-acting ones, such as phenobarbital, aren't too dangerous. By danger, I'm talking about addiction or need for the drug. The reason I mention this is because many people have children who are on phenobarbital. Doctors prescribe phenobarbital for the control of convulsions for some children who have a tendency toward this affliction. Its use is intended to control convulsive fits—not drug the mind. Phenobarbital, a slow-acting barbiturate, very rarely, if ever, becomes addictive.

On the other hand, people become highly addicted to fast-acting barbiturates. Some are so fast-acting that if I gave you a capsule and a glass of water, you'd be out in about ten minutes. You'd sleep about ten hours and then hardly even remember that I gave the drug to you. The Seconal and Nembutal aren't quite that fast-acting, but you can develop a tolerance to these. We haven't dwelt too much on tolerance yet, but it means developing a need for increasingly large amounts of a drug to get the same effect. You will see this increase in tolerance in mood-altering drugs, particularly sedatives.

I've skipped many drugs. There are obviously many more, but let's get to the real intent of this discourse on drugs. One drug I haven't mentioned yet is ALCOHOL. It's the easiest mood-altering drug to obtain and is probably the worst of all the drugs I've discussed here. Ethyl alcohol . . . you can buy it in practically any grocery or drugstore. Some people call it beer; some call it wine, whiskey, screwdrivers, martinis, et cetera. There are many names, but it's all alcohol. Alcohol is a sedative; it sedates the centers of the brain that control our actions. Some people comment, "What do you mean? I always have a ball on alcohol. I'm not as tonguetied," and so on. Well, the reason for that is the alcohol sedating those areas of the brain that made you a little inhibited. Once those brain areas lose their control over you, you become the uncontrolled person that you are trying chemically to be. That's the way it works, and that's why we drink, for the effect.

Alcohol is very dangerous. Typical of sedatives, alcohol kills. The way it kills? It kills when you come off it. That's why it's so bad—it kills you during withdrawal. I mentioned that most people who treat heroin addicts have never witnessed a death during withdrawal. On the contrary, physicians who work with alcoholics witness an alarmingly high death rate. In a hospital setting, the death rate is one out of twenty during alcohol withdrawal. In many acute-care hospitals, one of the highest death rates in the hospital occurs in the alcoholism-care unit. Even worse, one out of six alcohol addicts will die if they try to withdraw in a non-hospital setting.

In the hospital setting, although the drugs (sedatives) are not as strong as those used for coming off heroin, danger to your life is infinitely greater. Physicians try to control those symptoms by substituting (temporarily) another sedative to help you through withdrawal and to protect your life. The danger in withdrawal is that you may suffer what is called a central nervous system collapse. When your central nervous system is freed of the chemical sedation, alcohol (which is keeping it in check), you might turn to Jell-O. I've seen people die this way. In a central nervous system collapse (CNSC), you lose complete control of your body, i.e., the ability to move your muscles, hold your head up, and control your bodily functions. It's a very sad thing to watch. The publicized concept of the DTs (delirium tremens) is only one form of central nervous collapse.

Alcohol is also a debilitating drug. I mentioned that autopsies on people using opiates don't show much damage. On the contrary, people using alcohol exhibit all kinds of physical distress. They have heart damage, liver damage, metabolism and brain damage, and many other problems. Alcohol acts as a potentiating agent when combined with other drugs, in particular opiates or other sedatives. For example, one capsule of Librium may have the effect of six capsules when mixed with alcohol. Many so-called heroin overdose deaths are really the result of mixing heroin and alcohol in the body. The so-called Hollywood deaths involving celebrities are often due to the chemical reaction of sleeping pills and alcohol. As a rule, don't mix alcohol with other drugs.

In conclusion, I hope this talk has established in your mind the fact that alcohol is a serious drug, which should not be abused. Alcohol is very addictive, and of all the mood-altering drugs, ALCOHOL IS THE WORST KILLER.

FOUR CATEGORIES OF MOOD-ALTERING DRUGS

HALLUCINOGENS
(mind expanders)

- LSD (most common)
- PCP (angel dust/hog, easily manufactured)
- Mescaline/Peyote (ceremonies-southwest, not a great problem)
- THC (ingredient in marijuana, hard to extract)
- Marijuana (elevates pulse, can panic)
- Hashish (stronger than marijuana, a derivative of the same plant)

NON-ADDICTIVE
(can leave without difficulty)

NOT KILLERS
(philosophical argument, why?)

STIMULANTS
(tired? give a lift) (uppers)

- Nicotine—physical & psychological withdrawal
- Caffeine (feeling slow?)
- Dexedrine (reduce)
  Use became epidemic so D.E.A. reclassified as serious narcotic)
- Dexetrim (replaced dexedrine) consists of caffeine & decongestant
- Benzedrine (inhalers)
  Original serious abuse of amphetamines
- Amphetamines (speed freaks, suicide prone when come off)
- Cocaine/Crack
  Possibly classified as narcotic due to politics pressures

ADDICTIVE
DON'T DO A LOT
OF DAMAGE
SECONDARY KILLERS
(malnutrition/suicide prone)

OPIATES
(dreamers, narcotics, illegal)

- Morphine (pain killer)
  Physical & psychological; don't feel pain and don't want hassle. Most pleasant of human feelings, typical of all opiates
- Heroin (nat. & syn.)
  Very ill in withdrawal but no one dies
- Methadone (synthetic opiate)
  Assists in useful life off heroin
- Demerol—to get off heroin; pain killer in hospitals
- Percodan (medicinal, in-advertent addiction to this pain killer)

HIGHLY ADDICTIVE
It's a death sentence, but doesn't kill

SECONDARY KILLERS

SEDATIVES
(downers—when hyped up) Control neurosis-anxiety

- Valium (no. 1 in country)
- Librium (no. 3 in country)
  Both affect concentration—build mountains of mole-hills)
- Serex
- Mellaril
- Thorazine
  All 3 bad abuse potential
- Barbiturates (slow acting, useful in epilepsy; fast acting, dangerous)
- Seconal, Nembutal (develop tolerance) sleeping pills
- Alcohol
  Very dangerous when come off—can kill
  High withdrawal death rate
  Withdrawal usually requires substitute sedative

VERY ADDICTIVE
PRIMARY
KILLER

Talk 2

What Is Alcohol?

TYPES OF ALCOHOL (POISON)

CH$_3$CH$_2$OH—ethyl alcohol (ethanol)

CH$_3$OH—methyl alcohol (methanol)

CH$_3$CH$_2$CH$_2$OH—isopropyl alcohol

CH$_3$CH$_2$OH

CH$_3$CH$_2$CH$_2$OH   3.000 alcohols

CH$_3$OH

C—Carbon   H—Hydrogen   O—Oxygen

WHO DRINKS?

☆☆☆ Sample of Ten Adult Americans

Alcoholics   Problem drinkers   Social drinkers   Non-drinkers

ALCOHOL CONTENT OF DRINKS

Drink	Beer	Wine	Whiskey
Al. Range	3–6%	8–21%	40–75%
Average	5%	12%	43%
			86 proof
Serving Size	12 oz.	5 oz.	1.5 oz.
Al. Content	.6 oz.	.6 oz.	.65 oz.

BAL (BLOOD ALCOHOL LEVEL)

LEVEL %

.03	Impairment starts
.05	Social drinking limit
.07	Impaired driving (DIP)
.10	Drunk driving (DUIL)
.15	Problem drinkers
.40	Pass out
.60	DEATH

One 12 oz. beer raises BAL .024%.
150 lb. person gets rid of .015% per hour.

BAL level each hour if you drink
six-pack of 12 oz. beers in 3 hours

1 hr.	2 hrs.	3 hrs.
[1] [2]	[3] [4]	[5] [6]
.024	.033	.066
.024	.024	.024
.048	.024	.024
.048	.001	.114
.015	.015	.015
.033%	.066%	.099%
	(DIP)	(DUIL)

In Talk 1, we went through the various mood-altering drug categories in an attempt to show people where alcohol fits in with the mood-altering drugs. We concluded with a small discussion of what kind of a drug alcohol is and a few of the troubles you can have with it. Now I'd like to discuss what alcohol is, with the idea that it will help people who are having problems with alcohol to know the enemy and also help people who aren't having problems identify alcohol as a drug.

CHEMISTRY OF ALCOHOL

Some people think alcohol is food. It isn't. It's a drug. It's a chemical, and the chemical formula for alcohol is C_2H_5OH. For those who aren't familiar with chemistry:

- C is the symbol for carbon; diamonds are pure carbon.
- H is the symbol for hydrogen—a gas which is lighter than air. The big dirigible the *Hindenburg*, which blew up many years ago, was filled with hydrogen.
- O is the symbol for oxygen, and oxygen is the constituent in the air that we require for life. In hospitals, oxygen is identified by the color green, and the big green bottles there contain oxygen.

Another way of writing this is CH_3CH_2OH. You can see that there are two atoms of carbon, five atoms of hydrogen, and then the OH radical, which is called a hydroxide radical, consisting of an atom of oxygen and an atom of hydrogen. That particular combination is called *ethyl alcohol* or *ethanol*. Ethanol, among other things, is a poison. Ethyl alcohol or ethanol is better known as beer, wine, whiskey, et cetera. That's the type of alcohol we drink. There are about three thousand different alcohols. Ethyl alcohol is usually called *grain alcohol*.

Another common alcohol is CH_3OH, which is methanol or methyl alcohol. Some people call it wood alcohol. The race cars at the Indy 500 burn a blend of this alcohol as a fuel. They don't burn gasoline. Gasohol, which is gaining a great deal of publicity now, uses both ethyl alcohol and/or methanol mixed with gasoline.

Another common alcohol is CH_3CHCH_2OH, which is rubbing alcohol or isopropyl alcohol. The alcohol you buy from the drugstore to rub out soreness is isopropyl alcohol. Alcohol containing ethyl alcohol is also available for rubbing purposes. Drugstores sell this type of alcohol, but in order to sell it for other than drinking purposes, they have to add chemicals which make it unfit for drinking purposes. This is called denatured alcohol; the alcohol is taken out of its natural form. If you drank much of it, you'd become sick because it would irritate your stomach. That particular rubbing alcohol is about fifty to seventy percent alcohol by volume or 100 to 140 proof, so it would make a powerful drink—if you could drink it. You can buy a whole pint of it for about seventy-nine cents. Regardless of the formulation, rubbing alcohol is also a poison.

Additionally, $CH_3CH_4CH_4OH$ is an alcohol, $CH_3CH_2CH_5OH$ is an alcohol, et cetera. The thing which characterizes these alcohols is that they all begin with the CH_3 radical and all can be written with this hydroxide radical OH with different combinations of carbon and hydrogen in between.

You may wonder how we ended up drinking ethyl alcohol if we had a choice of three thousand alcohols. One of the reasons is that this particular form of alcohol is easily made. If you combine a fruit sugar with water, the yeast in the air will cause fermentation, and the result is ethyl alcohol. Of course, methyl alcohol or methanol is easily made, too. Wood chips allowed to ferment with a little yeast in water will make wood alcohol or methyl alcohol. Both are easily fermented. They're all poisons, but each will have a little different effect. Over thousands of years people have tried each one of these.

Let's say someone decided to have a party serving different kinds of these alcohols. He might say, "This fellow can drink this one. This gal will drink this one," et cetera, and he then tells everybody to drink up. The first two people who drink the alcohols $CH_3CH_2CH_9OH$ and $CH_3CH_2CH_5OH$ drop dead right away so everyone says, "We don't want that stuff." They cross those off the list. Somebody drinks CH_3CHCH_2OH and gets severe stomach cramps, so we cross that off. Someone drinks methanol. He has a pretty good party, but notices that he's beginning to lose his sight as the alcohol wears off. When the body breaks it down, this particular alcohol changes into formaldehyde. Formaldehyde is used for embalming dead bodies, so as one drinks methanol he is embalming himself. Formaldehyde also attacks the optic nerve. The person drinking ethyl alcohol probably has a pretty good time. If he drinks enough of it, he may feel a little bad the next day, but those bad feelings wear off in about twelve to twenty-four hours and he may be ready to go at it again. So why do people use it? Because its poisonous symptoms are less dramatic than those of the other alcohols. This is scarcely a recommendation, but we should keep in mind that it's a poison, though a more deceptive one than the other alcohols.

WHO DRINKS ALCOHOL?

Let's see who drinks this alcohol by looking at a random sample of ten adult Americans.

Don't Drink	Social Drinkers	Problem Drinkers	Alcoholics
(2)	(3)	(4)	(1)

Don't Drink
—Religious, social, family reasons or don't like
Social Drinkers
—Pace themselves .05 gr./100 cc.
Problem Drinkers
—Not social drinking because they're looking for an effect
Alcoholics
—Alcoholism is a disease—treatable but not curable

Two people don't drink alcohol because their religion forbids it. If you are a Mormon, Moslem, or Southern Baptist, your religion teaches you not to drink alcohol. There are also family reasons for not drinking alcohol. Some families frown on drinking, and they train their children accordingly. Other people may not drink because they don't like the effect they get from alcohol. This same effect is precisely why other people will drink. We're all a little different.

The next three out of ten are social drinkers, and this is where everyone thinks he is. You may have seen one of the big billboards put up by the National Council on Alcohol Abuse and Alcoholism which states that "if you have to drink to be social, that's not social drinking. . . ." and correctly so. This is an important fallacy believed by many people. They'll say, "When I'm at a party, I don't feel like talking unless I have a few drinks to loosen the tongue so I can be social." Well, that's not social drinking. That's drinking to drug yourself, to sedate those areas of the brain that are making you feel self-conscious, thereby freeing you from your inhibitions. That isn't social drinking, but most people claim to be social drinkers. Social drinkers rarely let their blood alcohol level go over .05 grams per 100 cubic centimeters of blood. (We'll discuss blood alcohol levels later, but that's about the level of social drinkers.) You might wonder—do they measure their blood alcohol when they're drinking? No, they can tell by the effect they get. They reach a certain blood alcohol level and stop drinking, or they pace themselves over a night of drinking. Now those five people out of ten, nondrinkers plus social drinkers, make up half the population.

On the other side of the line (the five out of ten remaining) are four people whom we'll call problem drinkers. In other words, forty percent of the adults in this country are problem drinkers. That's four out of the ten people. Problem drinkers consistently drink to blood alcohol levels of .15 grams per 100 centimeters of blood. They drink to that level because that's the effect they're looking for. Most problem drinkers are at this level when they're ready to go to the party, i.e., they're already feeling good. The severity of the drinking problem will vary, because if you're just over this line, obviously you're not a severe problem drinker. As you work yourself through this line, you find people drinking heavier and heavier.

Over here on the end is the oddball of the bunch, the alcoholic. One out of ten adult Americans is an alcoholic. Therefore, one out of eight people who drink ethyl alcohol is an alcoholic, because two of these people don't drink. You'll hear that statistic quoted quite frequently in discussions about alcoholism—the disease which afflicts alcoholics. It's a treatable but not a curable disease. This, then, is the pattern among people who drink alcohol.

People get into quite a quandary wondering whether they're problem drinkers or alcoholics. Although the alcoholic or problem drinker dilemma is discussed in Talk 5, let's dwell on that a bit now. Then we'll go on to some discussion of blood-alcohol levels.

First, let's expand on the problem drinker. The thing we notice about him is that a problem drinker can develop close to or, in most cases, a true, psychological addiction to alcohol. He thinks it's a habit, but it approaches a true psychological addiction. Addiction means need and he finds that there are many things he can't do without alcohol. He can't

24

function well. The way that his personality and mind operate demands alcohol. (This is also true of alcoholics.)

Alcoholics, however, develop a physical addiction to alcohol. I can say they develop or they possess. *Possess* is the key word. Alcoholics possess a physical addiction. Problem drinkers, apparently, don't become physically addicted. For alcoholics, the physical addiction manifests itself when they try to withdraw from alcohol after using it over a period of time. Symptoms of addiction, such as body tremors and various complaints, appear. That's a real feeling, because the body is demanding alcohol. In some cases, the person may die if he doesn't get alcohol or some other sedative. So there is a real need. Although problem drinkers consistently drink to blood alcohol levels of greater than .15 grams per 100 cc of blood, the amount that alcoholics drink varies widely. (Some people possess the disease of alcoholism but don't drink, so they never trigger the symptoms of the disease.) Although most alcoholics drink extremely large quantities, don't be deceived because you drink hardly anything. It could be any amount. Quantity has nothing to do with it. Unfortunately, there is no physiological test which can be given to people to determine whether or not they are alcoholics, but research is being carried on to determine if there is something in the blood that could be measured. However, psychological screening based on drinking habits can often screen out people who are alcoholics.

ALCOHOL CONTENT OF DRINKS

Let's set something straight: the quantities of alcohol we drink in certain sized glasses.

If I walked into a bar and the bartender gave me an ounce glass, poured beer in it, and said, "That'll be a buck," well, I'd probably say, "Wait a minute! This is the wrong glass," because beer doesn't come in that little one-ounce glass. It comes in a bigger glass or a mug. Well, there's a reason for that. Whiskey is served in a one-ounce glass because it runs anywhere from 86 to 100 proof or forty-three to fifty percent alcohol.

	Whiskey	Wine	Beer
Glass size (oz.)	1	4	8
Percent alcohol	43–50%	8–20%	4–8%
Oz. alcohol per drink	.5	.48	.48

You can buy stronger whiskeys. Ever Clear is a whiskey sold in thirty-eight of the fifty states which is about 190 proof or ninety-five percent alcohol. However, for the benefit of our discussion here, the usual whiskey is fifty percent alcohol. Fifty percent of one ounce of liquid in that glass is alcohol. So there is .5 ounce or ½ ounce of alcohol in one ounce of whiskey.

If I ordered a glass of wine, it would probably come in a four-ounce glass. The alcohol content of wine varies quite a bit from about eight to twenty percent. This would range from the so-called pop wines to fortified wines. The pop wines have a sweet taste and are designed to get young people off soda pop and onto alcohol. Many young people don't like alcohol, nor are they trained to handle it. Fortified wine, either port or sherry, has an alcohol content of twenty percent and was designed for so-called hard drinkers who like a little more bang to their drink. Because you can't reach that twenty percent alcohol level by natural fermentation, a little pure alcohol is added to reach the twenty percent level of fortified wines. Most of the wine in grocery stores is about twelve percent. Twelve percent of four ounces is .48 ounces, or for all practical purposes there is ½ an ounce of alcohol in a glass of wine.

Beer is served in an even larger, eight-ounce glass. The alcohol content of beer is somewhere between four and eight percent. Most beer is about six percent. Six percent of 8 ounces is .48 ounces, or, again, about ½ ounce of alcohol is in a glass of beer.

As you can see, you're really ordering a fixed amount of alcohol with a different flavor when you order different drinks. If drinking has become a problem, sometimes people will switch from whiskey to beer because they think beer is not as strong. However, they are only deceiving themselves, because beer isn't water and it has the same alcohol content as whiskey for a given size drink.

BLOOD ALCOHOL LEVELS

Let's get back to blood alcohol levels, since this concerns all drinkers. If you don't drink any alcohol, your blood alcohol level is zero. Please note that I say if YOU don't drink it, because rarely does anybody get thrown to the floor and have it poured down his throat. We do it ourselves and have to assume that responsibility. I mention this because some people who go before the judge will say, ''I don't know what happened. It must have been those grapes I ate—they fermented in my stomach and made me drunk.'' It doesn't work that way. If you don't drink alcohol, your blood alcohol level will be zero.

Impairment starts when the blood alcohol level reaches .03. This means grams of alcohol per 100 cc of blood or, since alcohol is close to water in weight, approximate percent of alcohol in the blood. One can of beer would take you a little below .03. Later, I'll express blood alcohol levels in terms of cans of beer. At a level of .03 percent, impairment can be determined by physical dexterity tests. A series of tests is given where you're flipping chalk, driving a car through pylons, or doing a simpler type of thing. The difference between a lower blood alcohol level and .03 percent level can be detected because at .03 percent you begin to get a little sloppy. When you reach about .05 percent, you have become progressively worse, although this is the level considered to be the social drinking limit.

The law states that you're guilty of impaired driving if you're driving a motorcar at .07 percent. In Utah and Idaho this is considered drunk driving or driving under the influence of liquor, but in the other forty-eight states it's considered impaired driving. At .1 percent, you're considered driving under the influence of liquor and you are a drunk driver. When you accept your driver's license from the secretary of state in Michigan, you agree or consent to a blood alcohol test if you are stopped by a police officer for suspicion of driving under the influence of alcohol. Usually, this is done with a breathalizer because it's more convenient, but it can be done with a blood sample, too. If you don't like that law, you can tell the secretary of state when you apply for your driver's license that you agree to take the driver's license but don't agree or consent to an alcohol test. In that event, you won't be issued a driver's license. Not much of an option, is it? If you don't like that law, get it changed. However, if you accept a driver's license, you have to agree to drive a motor vehicle according to that law, which is called the Implied Consent Law.

Problem drinkers, as I told you before, usually get up to a .15 percent blood alcohol level before they leave for a party. If you asked them about their condition, they'd probably say, ''Drunk, who's drunk? I'm not drunk—I'm just feeling good.'' So they drink on up to a blood alcohol level of about .4 percent and sedate themselves to a point where many of their brain functions are slowing or shutting down. They'll feel groggy and sleepy and near to passing out. Staggering around, they might say, ''I'm tired—I'd better go lie down. I think I'm drunk.'' Fortunately, we pass out when the blood alcohol level reaches .4 percent. Otherwise, the autonomic nervous system, which controls the heart and respiration, might shut down. This is death. It doesn't happen too often because people pass out before they reach this level. Now and then, you may read about someone who did reach that level, but it's usually the result of a chugalug contest. Someone says, "I can drink a fifth of vodka." Someone else says, "Show me." So he does and collapses about forty-five minutes later. An hour or so after that, he's dead. In this case, the blood alcohol level reaches .6 percent or higher. If there is someone there who is aware of what's happening, they can apply artificial means to keep the heart going in order to continue pumping oxygen into the body. Otherwise, the victim's respiration and heart will stop. At that time, you have about four minutes to get oxygen to the brain, or he'll become brain-damaged. After about six minutes he's dead, so you don't have much time. Such deaths aren't a common occurrence. You might say our bodies are programmed to save us; otherwise there would be more alcohol-related deaths.

BLOOD ALCOHOL LEVEL
EXPRESSED AS CANS OF BEER

Let's see what blood alcohol might mean in terms of cans of beer:

- One twelve-ounce beer consumed results in .024 percent BAL.*
- Rate at which body breaks down alcohol is .015 percent BAL per one hour.
- One hour after consuming a twelve-ounce beer the BAL is .009 percent.

So let's relate all this to a person who weighs 150 pounds—although this isn't too important. If he drinks a twelve-ounce can of beer, his blood alcohol content will rise to about .024 percent BAL about ten or fifteen minutes later. The body breaks down that poison, but it does so at a fairly fixed rate—at about .015 percent per hour.

Now let's drink a six-pack of beer over a period of three hours and see what happens. (If you drink it any faster, your blood alcohol levels will be higher than those given.) During the first hour, one can of beer raises your blood alcohol level to .024 percent. If you drink another quite rapidly, the blood alcohol level rises to .048 percent. A social drinker

*Blood alcohol level.

might say, "Well, that's it for the night." As a rule, social drinkers wouldn't drink that way—they would slowly drink a can of beer for an hour or so. You've probably been out with people who drink a highball or two cans of beer during the whole night. Most problem drinkers drink that much and more just to warm up. They say, "What's the point of drinking if you're only having two cans of beer?" They'll probably drink those pretty fast, so the blood level rises to .048 percent. They'll get rid of .015 percent, and so in the first hour they're at .033 percent or moderately impaired. Impairment starts there and after that it's mostly downhill. As they go into the next hour, they start at about a .033 percent blood alcohol level and then have another can of beer. The blood alcohol level rises to about .057 percent. Definitely, if you're a social drinker, that's it—three cans of beer in two hours. In fact, you're a little above the social drinker limit. The social drinker would call it an evening. If you can identify with that kind of drinking, you're a social drinker. If you feel you've only begun, you're not a social drinker; you have some type of problem. Now you have another beer, which takes us up to .081 percent, and you're getting rid of .015 percent for this hour, so you're at .066 percent at the end of two hours. That's impaired driving. If you drink four cans of beer in two hours and are stopped by a police officer while driving a motor vehicle, you can get hit with an impaired driving charge. If you go on into the third hour starting at .066 percent, have two more cans of beer, making this .114 percent, and get rid of .015 percent, you'll end up with .099 percent BAL. For all practical purposes this is drunk driving.

So we can say that if you drink two cans of beer an hour (or a six-pack over a three-hour period), you will be legally drunk at the end of three hours. Most people don't realize this, because if you're a problem drinker you aren't where you want to be yet. You aren't even at .15 percent yet. Chances are a problem drinker would drink five cans of beer or five shots of whiskey that first hour. This would take him up to .120 percent, and at the end of that first hour he would be at .1 percent. We find people gulping drinks, but if you've a problem with alcohol and the law you should become aware of blood alcohol levels or your legal problems may escalate.

Summarizing this talk, we have learned that alcohol is a chemical that shows up in our blood in different concentrations, depending on how much we drink over a period of time. Knowing about alcohol removes some of the mystery and fear associated with its use and therefore places any discussion of this drug in its proper perspective.

Talk 3

Physical Damage from Alcohol

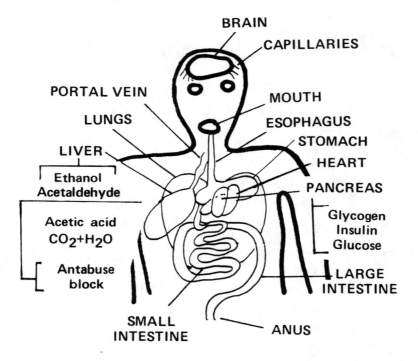

BRAIN

CAPILLARIES

PORTAL VEIN

MOUTH

LUNGS

ESOPHAGUS

LIVER

STOMACH

Ethanol
Acetaldehyde

HEART

PANCREAS

Acetic acid
$CO_2 + H_2O$

Glycogen
Insulin
Glucose

Antabuse
block

LARGE
INTESTINE

SMALL
INTESTINE

ANUS

The first thing we do with alcohol is pour it in our mouths. We could pour it in our ears, inject ourselves, or rub it on our skin, but we pour it in our mouths. As I mentioned before, we're responsible for pouring it in our mouths. Rarely is anyone thrown to the floor and alcohol poured down his throat. After we pour the alcohol into our mouth, it enters the throat, then drops down through the esophagus into the stomach. It actually makes a splash when it lands in the stomach. If you've ever seen flouroscopic displays of someone drinking barium, you've seen the barium drop down and sort of splash when it enters the stomach, too. Now the alcohol is in the stomach and we're in trouble.

DISORDERS OF MOUTH, ESOPHAGUS, STOMACH, INTESTINE

A few things are already beginning to happen. Let me explain that the inside of the mouth, esophagus, and stomach are all lined with mucus. A primary purpose of this mucus is to protect the tissue from irritants, and alcohol is a relatively severe irritant. For instance, if you drink a shot of whiskey, you might say, "Wow, that stuff burned all the way down." That's because it has irritating properties. Alcohol dilutes the mucus which lines the inside of the mouth. In doing that, it removes the protective barrier which normally serves to protect the flesh from this irritant. Microscopic holes in that mucus develop into microscopic sores inside your mouth and down into your esophagus and stomach. Usually, these sores heal very rapidly—like a cut on your finger. The wound begins to heal because cells form over it. When you cut your finger, a scab forms which covers the wound. When the wound has healed, the scab sloughs off and falls away. The same thing happens inside the mouth. The microscopic sores caused by the irritation of alcohol are covered by the formation of cells to close off the wound. After the wound is covered, these cells stop multiplying or growing and the wound eventually heals itself. Over a short period of time, this will not cause a problem. However, we're beginning to find that something else happens in people (particularly men and women in their forties and fifties) who use alcohol for a long period of time. It is suspected that these little sores begin to repeat in the same place during a period of time. Eventually, the cells which are covered by the scab don't stop multiplying. The cells continue growing until a mutation occurs called *cancer*.

We suspect that one of the leading causes of cancer of the mouth is abuse of alcohol. This same type of cancer occurs down through the esophagus and stomach. This type of cancer, like all cancers, is readily curable in the early stages, but unfortunately, this type isn't detected in the early stages. People tend to attribute their discomfort to a sore throat which "just keeps hanging on." Or, if they're drinking much, alcohol anesthetizes the soreness so they're not concerned about it. Actually, it's cancer of the mouth or esophagus and eventually it will spread to other parts of the body. Many people don't go to their doctor with this condition, and once this type of cancer reaches a point where it's difficult to cure, it will usually kill in about a year or a year and a half, in spite of chemotherapy and cobalt treatments.

In the stomach you can get a similar type of cancer, plus some other things. The stomach really sits quite high up on the body. It's almost covered by the rib cage off to the center left of the body. I mention this because when the doctor asks where it hurts, many people who complain of a stomachache mistakenly point to their intestines. Your stomach is up quite high. The mucus in the stomach has to be quite thick because part of the activity of the stomach is to mix hydrochloric acid with food to break it down. Hydrochloric acid is very potent. For example, if I were pouring hydrochloric acid on this table, it would burn a hole in the wood. The primary protection your stomach has from hydrochloric acid is mucus. As alcohol dilutes that mucus, you may then get holes in the covering which protects the stomach and sores will form. Usually, the type of people who get these sores from alcohol become aware of them because of stomach pains. The sores are very painful because they're like a raw wound, and often people will try to kill that pain by drinking more alcohol. Many people in hospitals have these sores, more commonly known as ulcers.

A typical dialogue with a patient might be something like this:

"Can't you get me out of here?"

"Why?"

"Well, the doctor isn't giving me anything to kill that pain. I've got to get out of here and get a drink—to get rid of that pain in my stomach.''

In reality, the doctor is trying to lower the stomach acidity. With a restricted diet and given time, the pain will go away as the stomach is able to heal itself. However, it's not instantaneous and without treatment ulcers develop.

Ulcers can also develop in the outlet from the stomach to the small intestine, which is called the duodenum. If untreated, this type of ulcer will bleed, and the blood will begin to accumulate a little in the stomach. Blood doesn't digest too well, so you become nauseated and throw it up. Then you become alarmed and go to the hospital. Fortunately, doctors are very successful at stopping that type of bleeding and there is a good chance of recovery. However, from then on you will have to watch your use of alcohol. Extreme caution is called for, because this type of wound can turn into cancer, too.

Next we come to the intestines. Food begins to work its way down from the small intestine into the large intestine. The small intestine is very long, and because it is convoluted, it has a great deal of surface area. It's like looking at a radiator hose in a car—or some type of flexible hose. The food works its way down where it is broken down and leaves the intestine in the form of glucose. The food then enters the bloodstream in the form of glucose, which is sugar. This is how we nourish ourselves. The residue, of course, works itself down until it reaches the end of the small intestine, passes through a little valve-like mechanism and then enters the large intestine. The large intestine sort of loops backward and up in what we call the ascending colon to the transverse colon and then the descending colon to the anal area. We don't have much trouble in the small intestine because a great deal of food is being broken down in there, but a problem develops in the large intestine if we've been drinking alcohol. Ethyl alcohol, perhaps methanol, and some of the simpler alcohols diffuse through the stomach wall into the bloodstream without much of it entering the intestine. However, trace amounts of the other three thousand more complex alcohols that I mentioned will begin to work their way down through the large intestine in minute amounts. Some of these settle in the pockets or convolutions, particularly toward the end of the large intestine. This causes a localized irritation. If these irritants settle in the valve-like mechanism which connects the small and large intestines, ileitis can develop. If the irritants remain in the large intestine, they cause colitis. If they proceed even farther into the colon area, diverticulitis results. All of these are painful and very annoying sicknesses, and it is thought that a great deal of this is attributable to the inordinate use of alcohol. Once again, though, this type of irritation can be cured.

If you have a serious problem in the colon, pus and soreness will result. The solution for this may be an operation which blocks off the colon and reroutes it through your abdominal wall to a little bag. The residue from the colon then drops in that bag. You won't have to worry about going to the toilet, but most people find this unpleasant and distasteful. If the lower part of the colon heals, the colon can be reconnected and the bag removed. However, you'll have to be careful about drinking alcohol or using other irritants again.

Some people reach a stage where the constant irritation turns into cancer. The very fortunate have this detected early—the cancerous tissue can still be removed, and if necessary, a bag can be hung permanently on the side of the body. Even though they have the inconvenience of that bag, at least they are surviving. The less fortunate (and there are many) go around undetected and suffering. Once it has developed, the cancer will kill you within four to six months, so it's nothing to fool around with. If you're having any problems in the stomach area or through the small or large intestine, I would like to suggest that you be very careful about how much alcohol you drink. Otherwise, you'll further aggravate your problem.

METABOLIC DISORDERS AND THE PANCREAS

I mentioned that when our food leaves the intestine it enters the bloodstream in the form of glucose. After all the cells in our body have received a sufficient amount of nourishment, any excess glucose not converted to fat is turned into a substance called *glycogen*. Glycogen is stored in the liver, which is a relatively large organ—in fact, it's the largest organ in the body. In a cross-section comparison, it's about the size of my hand, about the same thickness, and weighs anywhere from five to seven pounds. One of the functions of the liver is to store glycogen in the liver cells. This stored energy or glycogen is released by the liver as it is needed, and the glycogen then stimulates the pancreas.

The pancreas is an organ about the size of the thumb and is located behind the stomach, where it secretes a hormone called insulin. This insulin combines with the glycogen and converts the glycogen back to glucose in our bloodstream so we can nourish ourselves.

36

BLOOD ALCOHOL IMPAIRMENT SCALE
(Determined by breathalizer or blood sample)

	Grams per 100 cc of blood or approximate %
Normal	0
Impairment begins (determined by physical dexterity)	.03
Social drinker	.05
Law says driving impaired	.07
Driving under the influence of liquor	.10
Problem drinkers (before leaving for party)	.15
Staggering, passing out (body programmed to save us)	.40
Chugalug	.60
Death (autonomic nervous system shuts down)	.60

When I talk about the process of converting glycogen into glucose with the help of insulin, I should mention that some people develop a condition called *hypoglycemia*. Hyperglycemia means a large amount of sugar in the blood, but hypoglycemia means a low amount of sugar in the blood. Hyperglycemia is called *diabetes*; hypoclycemia is usually known as *low blood sugar* and classified as a functional disorder. In hypoglycemia, the mechanism which controls the amount of glycogen being released by the liver into the bloodstream (to be broken down by insulin into glucose) goes haywire. Normally, we produce insulin to break down the glycogen, converting it to a given amount of glucose, and the body stabilizes itself. However, if you have hypoclycemia, the production of insulin continues after the body has a sufficient amount of glucose. Insulin continues to be produced by the pancreas. Eventually, the insulin will use up all of the glycogen in your bloodstream and begin to deplete the glycogen in your liver quite seriously, which then drives the blood sugar level down. This will cause your brain to starve for sugar and gives you a very peculiar feeling. If you use alcohol and have this condition of hypoglycemia, alcohol will trigger this condition. As your liver cells mobilize to break down the poison, alcohol, large amounts of glycogen are released. The insulin begins pumping again, and you'll have trouble stopping it. If you use alcohol over a period of time and abuse it, you may interfere with this mechanism to the point where you become hypoglycemic. This is very common in alcoholics.

First hour	Second hour	Third hour
2 cans of beer	2 cans of beer	2 cans of beer
.024%	.033% BAL (start)	.066% BAL (start)
+.024	.024	.024
.048% BAL	+.024	+.024
−.015% per hour	.081	.114
.003 BAL	−.015 (breaks down)	−.015
	.066% BAL	.099% BAL

At one time it was thought that hypoglycemia was the cause of alcoholism. The hypoglycemic person was thought to drink alcohol in an attempt to maintain an adequate supply of glycogen for conversion of the excessive secreted insulin into glucose. This eventually becomes self-defeating as the glycogen supply is depleted. However, it has been found that all alcoholics are not suffering from hypoglycemia and vice versa. So although people with drinking problems should be cautious about developing hypoglycemia and the incidence is high in alcoholics, this is not the sole cause of alcoholism.

Another thing I should mention is that the pancreas has little islets on it. Under a microscope, these weird-looking things look like little volcanoes. They're called islets of Langerhans. There is much we don't know about the pancreas, but we do know that these islets secrete insulin, which (among other things) has something to do with diabetes. Up to 1929, diabetes was tantamount to a death sentence. In 1929, it was discovered in Canada that diabetes could be controlled with insulin from the pancreas of a pig. The little islets are delicate and become irritated from inordinate overuse. When irritated, they are painful and some people develop a condition called pancreatitis. This is such a painful condition that it has been described as possibly the worst type of pain that a human being can experience. In our hospitals, people with pancreatitis have to be given large amounts of a painkiller, such as Demerol, to lower the pain level. Fortunately, pancreatitis is usually self-regulating and can heal itself in four or five days. However, again, it's like any part of the body, and constant irritation can cause tumors to develop in the pancreas. Many of these tumors are malignant or cancerous, and that particular type of tumor is very deadly. It's a very fast-growing tumor. People who develop cancer of the pancreas expire in less than a month, before they're even diagnosed. Usually, the autopsy is what reveals the cause of death. Again, that is mainly due to overstimulating the pancreas through the inordinate use of alcohol.

Hypoglycemia itself is caused by overindulgence in sugar, and abusing alcohol may be the straw that breaks the pancreas. Most people are not aware of this serious threat to their health. A separate talk will be given on this subject.

LIVER DISORDERS

Alcohol, being a poison, has to be broken down in the body and the liver is the organ which performs this function. So after we drink the alcohol, it splashes into the stomach, where about ninety-five percent of it passes through the stomach wall into the bloodstream. It then courses all through the body. Alcohol is not a selective drug. It's found in slightly higher concentrations in some parts of the body, but it reaches all points of the body. For all practical purposes you might say that you have as much alcohol in your little toe as you have in the top of your head.

In coursing through the body, the alcohol passes through a series of blood vessels located in the chest area, which supply a vein called the portal vein, which supplies blood to the liver. Every time blood circulates through your body, it passes through this portal vein into the liver. If there are poisons in what we drink, the liver is mobilized to break them down. Because alcohol is a poison, the liver acts to immobilize it by releasing glycogen from the liver cells. This is why people get a jolt of energy after they've had a couple of drinks. They'll say, "Boy, that really picked me up." This isn't only a psychological reaction; it's a physiological effect, because you're giving yourself an infusion of glycogen and the insulin level of your body is rising. As a result, the glucose level will rise so you'll have more energy.

Once the glycogen leaves the liver cells, the cells begin to break down the alcohol. The alcohol enters the liver, where it combines with an enzyme called alcohol dehydrogenase.

There are different kinds of enzymes in our body, and you can think of them as catalysts. This alcohol dehydrogenase acts as a catalyst by breaking down the alcohol and turning it into acetaldehyde, which is very poisonous, and the body rapidly converts it into acetic acid. (Vinegar is diluted acetic acid.) The acetic acid then changes to carbon dioxide (that fizzy stuff in soda pop), which is eliminated from our bodies, thereby completing the process of breaking down poisonous alcohol. It's a very interesting process that, unfortunately, we never think about while we're drinking. For instance, if we were drinking methyl alcohol, it would change into formaldehyde (embalming fluid) instead of acetaldehyde. That's the danger with methyl alcohol.

Acetaldehyde, as a poison, is being investigated by researchers. It's been theorized that certain people may have a naturally high level of acetaldehyde in their bodies, which is linked to their brain function. Consequently, these individuals learn to function in a so-called poisonous state. They learn to cope psychologically and physiologically with the feelings they get from these relatively high acetaldehyde levels. When that level begins to fall off, they want to take something which will raise it again so they feel normal. Of course, the way to do that is to take some ethyl alcohol to supposedly feel better. If this theory can be proven by researchers, a simple blood test for normal acetaldehyde level could determine whether people are alcoholics. That would be an aid in the medical diagnosis of alcoholism.

Also, another interesting thing occurs here. When I described how glycogen with the use of insulin breaks down into glucose, we also touched on another very common problem—the disease called diabetes. In a simplified sense, people who don't have a naturally sufficient supply of insulin in their bodies develop a disease called *diabetes* because they can't convert the glycogen in their bloodstream into glucose—therefore, they can't nourish themselves. It's thought that there are hormones, other than insulin, which help this process out. While looking for some of these so-called oral medications for use with diabetes, in Denmark about thirty years ago a drug called disulfiram was produced. It wasn't very helpful to diabetes, but in the course of studying it something else of interest was noted. It was observed that the transformation of alcohol from acetaldehyde to acetic acid is blocked by disulfiram. If this transformation cannot occur, the individual becomes deathly ill, because acetaldehyde is a strong poison. He becomes so ill that his body goes into shock. Well, researchers thought this would be a panacea for people with problem drinking occurrences or alcoholics. They could be given this drug, and if they drank alcohol, they would become very sick; it would be an aversion-type therapy. The commercial name given to this drug is Antabuse (anti–alcohol abuse), and it is very effective. If you have a sufficient amount of Antabuse in your body and drink one-half of a glass of beer, you'll become deathly ill. There is a very fast reaction. When used properly, it is very effective. However, if improperly used, Antabuse can cause a return to drinking. A separate talk will be given on Antabuse due to the importance of this subject.

Back to the digestive system. The liver now comes in contact with the acetaldehyde, which, being very toxic and poisonous, kills liver cells. When those liver cells are killed, the cell becomes infused with a fatty substance called triglyceride, which surrounds the liver cells and generally lines the liver. That fat will occupy the liver cells, and as it does, the liver begins to enlarge. We develop what is called *a fatty liver*. When you see the doctor, he may say, "How much have you been drinking?" You reply, "Oh, doc, I have a couple of beers a day." The doctor is probably thinking to himself, *Why, you lying fool, you've been drinking a fifth a day to have a liver like that.* Your liver is all fatty and enlarged. Some people get such a large liver that their abdomen begins to stick out on the right side. Consequently, a great deal of fluid collects in the abdominal cavity because the liver isn't functioning right and the body's fluid balance is out of kilter. The abdominal cavity begins to swell and sometimes has to be tapped in the hospital. A quart or so of fluid is drawn off with a plunger. This is usually due to a fatty liver. It's been estimated that if you drink about four bottles of beer a day for eleven days (which isn't a heck of a lot of beer), you'll begin to develop a fatty liver. Fortunately, if you stay away from alcohol or other poisons (primarily alcohol), that fatty liver can rejuvenate itself. The liver is the only major organ in the body that can do this. The fat will gradually leave the liver, and in one to two years the liver cells become vital and active again. So we're lucky.

However, many people with a fatty liver continue drinking, and eventually the liver cells are so badly damaged that they won't even contain fat anymore. They develop into hard spots on the liver, and the liver may even shrink a little due to these hard spots. That's called cirrhosis of the liver—hardened areas on the liver. A liver removed from a person with cirrhosis during an autopsy looks like a piece of beef liver left out in the air overnight. It's sort of deep red and glistening when you put it out, but it turns an orange-chocolaty color with hard spots all over it. Those hard spots can be removed surgically—that's called *barbering the liver*. Fortunately, we have about three times as much liver as we need to live, so you can destroy about two-thirds of your liver and still function. You won't have much energy, because you can't store a lot of glycogen, but you can function. That's why some people get away with cirrhosis of the liver for years before death occurs.

Now we have to think about what's happening with this blood coming through the portal vein. As I mentioned before, it's fed by blood vessels running down the throat and chest area. If there are many hard spots here in the liver and if all of the blood in your body has to go through your liver, the blood has to build up pressure upstream of the liver. What happens is that these little blood vessels begin to expand and stick out. In people with bad cases of cirrhosis of the liver, you can detect those blood vessels standing out on the chest from that pressure. That's not too serious. What's really bad is that these blood vessels begin to stick out in the esophagus. This usually goes hand in hand with a very bad mucous lining in the esophagus (from alcohol—an irritated esophagus). The esophagus is a very irregular tube. When the blood vessels stick out (very close and exposed), they spring leaks. As a result, blood starts leaking into the stomach, and actually, you are bleeding to death. Sometimes it's more dramatic than that. You may suddenly suffer a massive rupture of a blood vessel in the esophagus and hemorrhage very rapidly. On one occasion, a twenty-one-year-old fellow undergoing hospitalization for cirrhosis of the liver suffered such an attack. He was talking with a nurse when all of a sudden he hemorrhaged in the esophagus. He sprayed her and the inside of the room with blood. Nothing could be done for him—he died very rapidly.

Usually, it doesn't happen that suddenly. You may go to the hospital because you don't feel well. It's determined you're bleeding and leaking blood into the stomach, so now the race is on to save your life. Because you're bleeding to death, coagulants are given to try to stop the bleeding, i.e., close up those wounds. As a rule, a blood transfusion is given, too, because you're losing so much blood. You'll receive about fifteen pints of blood, and it will leak into your bladder and everywhere. So much blood is lost that eventually it can't be controlled. One of the last resorts is to place a balloon-like bag in the esophagus which when inflated (if successful) will press on the sides of the esophagus to stop the bleeding. Surgically, it's almost impossible to stop the bleeding. Because esophagal bleeding is a common problem, research is being carried on to minimize it. For instance, a hospital in Florida is trying to develop techniques to stop esophagal bleeding. However, at this time all the doctor can do is put you back in your bed and call your family. When your family arrives, you aren't in much pain. You can converse for a while, but you gradually become weak because your blood level is getting so low that the brain becomes starved for glucose. Nothing can be done for you. This causes a coma, and death follows shortly after.

That's death from cirrhosis of the liver, and the most common way of dying from cirrhosis of the liver is to bleed to death. Records are fairly accurate on these deaths, and it's estimated that ninety-five percent of the cases of cirrhosis of the liver in this country are caused by the abuse of alcohol. That affliction is the seventh leading cause of death in this country, which means that there are many deaths from the abuse of alcohol.

DISORDERS OF THE BRAIN

Something else is also happening when we drink alcohol. Triglycerides are released into the bloodstream from the liver. These triglycerides are little globules or spheres of fat. They get into the bloodstream and travel through the body. Perhaps you have heard of cholesterol as a form of fat or plaque in our blood vessels. Similarly, we get these triglycerides in our bloodstream from drinking alcohol. The brain is nourished by many little capillaries entering the brain which carry glucose and oxygen to the brain cells. These little capillaries become very, very tiny—they really narrow down. If you have an excess of these little globules of triglycerides in your bloodstream, they begin to accumulate in the ends of the capillaries and plug them up so the blood can't get through. When this happens, the brain cells to be nourished by these capillaries begin to die. The result: dead brain cells. Every time we drink alcohol, we kill brain cells, but we have billions of them so normally we don't notice this change. Unlike the liver cells, the brain cells don't become fatty, or perhaps many of us would have fat heads. However, they do begin to collect a watery substance. Instead of scattering through various areas of the brain, over a period of time these cells tend to congregate into patches of destroyed brain cells. They're wet, jelly-like patches in the brain and are referred to in layman's language as *wet brain*. Generally, wet brain occurs in people who are in their mid-fifties or older and have used alcohol for a period of twenty or thirty years.

Talking to a person with this condition is a peculiar experience because they have lucid moments. In other words, they will converse with you and everything seems to be all right, but suddenly they will lapse into gibberish because the brain isn't functioning properly. They don't know where they are or who they're talking to and could care less; they become vegetable-like. The family is quite concerned because they never know when these periods will occur. As a result, you can't have these people in the streets, so you must hospitalize them. In other words, people with wet brain can be considered psychotic or insane. Although they have periods of insanity, they aren't violent or dangerous to others. However, they are dangerous to themselves, so they cannot live in a normal environment. Usually, the doctor advises the family to take the matter up in court and testifies to the medical condition of the patient. The family obtains a court order to commit the person to a state mental institution. I've seen it many times. The family comes to the hospital with a court order, and they'll drive the patient to the state institution. Sometimes the sheriff comes, but either way, it's a sad thing to see. It's been estimated that forty to sixty percent of the people in mental hospitals have been institutionalized due to wet brain. That's a tremendously high statistic, especially when you consider that wet brain is caused by the abuse of alcohol. Now I would suppose that when they're in a psychotic state these people do not care about being patients in a state hospital. But I know they have lucid moments when knowing they're confined until death must be a terrible burden. It's probably very tough on them.

It's thought that this type of thing also accounts for what are called *blackouts* and memory lapses of alcoholics. A person may go on a drinking spree and later not remember what he did for a period of time. That period may vary from ten minutes to ten weeks or ten months. It is not uncommon for drinkers to be arrested for a crime which they can't remember. It is thought that the memory cells which record data while it is transpiring have been destroyed and consequently the mind can't recall what happened. A young fellow in jail recently is a classic example of this problem. He awoke there one morning and made a big commotion. When the police responded, he said he knew why he was there but wanted to call his mother so she wouldn't worry about him. The policeman said,

"Well, son, you don't have to worry about your mother. You're here because you shot and killed her last night." The man didn't even remember it. That must be a terrible circumstance. Many people become involved in traffic accidents or fights which they can't remember the next day. Because there are other witnesses to the crime, they are sent to prison, never remembering what happened. Blackouts can cause that. It's been pretty well determined that if you suffer blackouts you're probably an alcoholic. It's one of the characteristics of alcoholism and potential wet brain.

HEART DISORDERS

Now the next matter at hand is your heart. It is a really large muscle which sits up in the center of the chest and consists of four chambers and four valves. For some reason, alcohol breaks down muscle tissue. We don't know why. If we were making an in-depth examination here, I could show you slides of heart tissue taken from people who were known abusers of alcohol and people who weren't. You could see the actual destruction of the muscle tissue. Alcohol breaks down muscle tissue throughout the body, but the large muscle that we are concerned about is the heart. It beats in a regular sinus cycle: periodic rhythm pumps a fixed amount of blood, speeds up, and slow down. If you drink alcohol, heart muscle is affected to the extent that your heart will gallop and you'll develop what is called a *galloping heart*. We can see this in many people, not necessarily alcoholics, but it's thought to account for many of the sudden deaths of people who have been drinking. They collapse and die. As the heart gallops, it can begin to fibrillate and quiver. When it's quivering, that muscle can't pump any blood to restore itself to a normal sinus rhythm—like a bowl of Jell-O, that's fibrillation. When your heart stops pumping blood effectively, it has the effect of carrying a five-hundred-pound sack of potatoes on your back. You'll drop pretty fast. That's how rapid it is. If there's someone around who can detect the problem and restore your heartbeat, you're all right. If there isn't, you'll expire. Besides this sudden death possibility, we also see destruction to the heart muscle in people drinking alcohol over a period of time. Eventually, their hearts won't pump effectively and, as the muscle weakens, congestive heart failure develops, which seriously limits your activities.

45

If your condition becomes serious, only a heart transplant can save you, and they haven't been very successful. You won't have a sudden heart attack, but your heart is worn out, so it no longer functions as a muscle should. This leads to cardiovascular problems and heart disease, which is the number one killer. So once again, alcohol is responsible for many deaths.

LUNG DISORDERS

The lungs are also tied into that heart action, because as we develop a weakened or galloping heart condition, a little fluid begins to accumulate in the lungs. It settles in the lungs, and people who use alcohol quite often accumulate fluid in the bottom of their lungs. That fluid is like stagnant water. When we breathe, the fluid is exposed to the air, which contains germs, bacteria, and whatnot. The germs and bacteria multiply in the solution at the bottom of the lungs. This condition is thought to be one of the reasons why many alcoholics persistently have upper respiratory infections. They have bronchitis, sinus problems, sore throats, or colds, and they only seem to recover from one infection when they catch another. They may change from one antibiotic to another, but they'll never be rid of those chronic problems until their body condition is returned to a healthy state. To develop good heart action and good blood flow they'll have to stay away from alcohol. Otherwise they'll be plagued with these infections and may eventually develop pneumonia.

If you're young and contract bacterial pneumonia, you've a good chance of pulling through. However, when you reach the age of seventy or so, pneumonia becomes a tremendous killer. In particular, viral pneumonia will probably kill you, because it's caused by a virus and you have a weakened lung condition. There is no antibiotic to kill that virus, and the body has to fight it off. So both viral and bacterial pneumonias can be killers and the age of death from pneumonia drops down into the forties, fifties and sixties for people who continually abuse alcohol.

Another symptom of alcoholism is the breakdown of tissue on the surface skin. Some people who drink alcohol develop a wax-like or transluscent skin. They seem to have a cellophane film plastered over their skin—like a film over flesh—and there seems to be no depth to their skin. Most, but not all, of these people are alcohol abusers.

To sum things up, there may be other little problems, but these are the major ones. A person who abuses alcohol develops problems in all of these areas. Autopsies performed on alcoholics show that the body actually degenerates. There is no question that alcohol is a seriously debilitating drug if consumed in any quantity and should be used with a proper degree of caution—if one wants to maintain a healthy body.

Talk 4

Alcohol and Learned Behavior

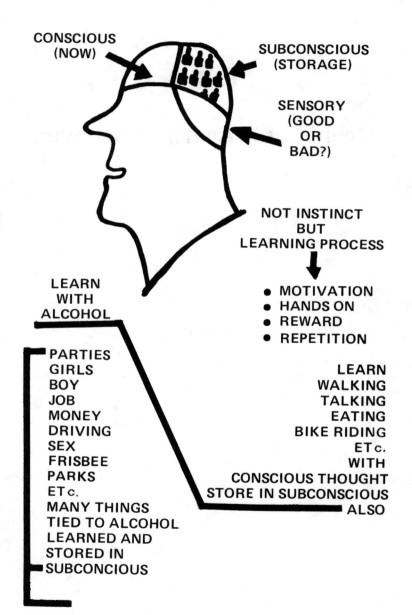

It has been suggested that the abuse of alcohol is a behavior problem. Let us make a simplified analysis of learned behavior as it relates to alcohol.

LEARNING PROCESS

Human beings, contrary to popular belief, learn how to do things rather than do things instinctively. As infants, we are relatively helpless compared to various animals. We must be fed, clothed, kept warm or cool, nursed, and be completely provided for in all areas of our existence for many years. We are taught to learn how to do things, and once we learn, we never seem to forget what we learn.

We learn by a certain process which can be thought of as consisting of the following steps:

1. MOTIVATION
2. HANDS-ON
3. REWARD
4. REPETITION

Let's apply these steps to the simple task of learning to ride a bicycle. As youngsters, we may be motivated to ride a bike by the fact that other kids are doing it or that it may be a nice way to travel compared with walking. Therefore, MOTIVATION is our reason for doing something. We actually learn how to ride a bike by getting on a bike and attempting to ride it without falling over. This is the HANDS-ON process of actually doing something. It would be difficult to learn to ride a bike by reading about bike riding. A person must actually ride the bike. Hands-On is the process of learning by doing something, i.e., experiencing what you're trying to do. Our first REWARD, if we're riding a bicycle, would be merely to be able to ride it or the sense of accomplishment that we get because no one is holding it up for us. Later there will be other rewards;

for instance, we can get around faster and we enjoy riding it. When we begin we can hardly ride the bike, but after a few months we can ride it without any hands and do all kinds of tricks. That's all due to REP-ETITION. All that information, of course, we learn. If we haven't ridden a bike for ten or twenty years, we'll find that we're able to hop right on and ride away because we had learned how to do this. We may have to upgrade our skills a little, but we'll never forget how to ride a bike—and that's true of almost everything.

LEARNING STORAGE

For our purposes in this talk think of the brain as having three areas. The frontal area represents the conscious area of the brain. The rearward area of the brain we call the subconscious, and the third area is the sensory part of the brain (which tells us if we like or dislike something). Getting back to that bicycle, the idea of trying to ride the bike appears in the conscious area of the brain and provides motivation so we consciously experience riding the bike. We're aware of that in the conscious part of the brain. Next we begin to store information about riding the bike back in the subsconscious. The reward comes from examining what we're doing in the sensory part of the brain. Here we decide whether we like or dislike it and store that information also in the subconscious. Of course, the more we repeat this experience of riding a bike, the more information we're storing in the subconscious about riding a bike. Now we always possess that information. Some people may have better recall than others, but all of us possess the ability to store this information. We possess it to a greater degree than any computer.

Let's take a look at alcohol again, using a few examples to show how it fits in with our problem. We could say I'm a young person, perhaps a teenager, and I'm going to a party. My mind begins to process this information. I formulate the idea to go to a party in the conscious part of the brain, then ask the subconscious if the subconscious has any information on parties. If I'm very young, I might not have much infor-mation on parties. However, my subconscious may tell me, *Look, you might enjoy it once you go to that party*. So I go to the party and perhaps

I don't have a very good time. Perhaps I'm shy or a little introverted or I don't know what to do with myself in that experience. I may not have a very good time, and I'll store the information that parties aren't much fun. However, I may have noticed that other teenagers brought along a few bottles of beer and they seemed to be having a good time. So I store the information that perhaps parties with a little alcohol are fun. Now I may not think about that again until I am invited to another party. Again I go back into my subconscious, and it says, *Well, parties are no fun*, but I have another little bit of information there on parties which says, *Perhaps parties with a little beer might be fun*. So I decide, *I'll go to the party, and if I'm not having fun, I'll have a couple of beers with the kids*. So I do that and, perhaps, have a good time because that beer contains ethyl alcohol, which sedates the areas of the brain which are causing me to be inhibited. Removing some of those inhibitions sometimes allows me to enjoy myself more. Without really knowing it, I've drugged myself. Now all that information, whether it's good or bad, is weighed in the sensory part of the brain and stored in the subconscious. In the following examples, let's forget about the sensory process and concentrate on what we're storing in our subconscious.

We're ready now for a third experience or party, and so far we have three bits of information: 1) parties are no good, 2) parties with beer might be fun, and 3) parties with beer are a good time. Another party using alcohol raises that to four bits of information, and if I continue to drink and attend parties, I will become a forty-year-old adult who has stored a substantial amount of information in the brain about parties and alcohol.

To continue my example, when I grow up, I may marry. Marriage is a difficult situation at best because you're working with two individuals. Everyone has different ideas, and you have to make many compromises. Problems come up in marriage, and some people get pretty upset. During an argument, the husband may say to himself, *Arguing with the wife is no fun. I know that because I've experienced it before*, and leave the house in a huff for the bar and a calming drink. The wife thinks, *I'm glad the son of a bitch is gone, but gee, I'm so nervous and uptight I don't know what to do with myself.* (We don't like that antagonism.) So she decides, *Maybe I'll have a little drink to calm me down.* Both get the calming effect of the sedation from the alcohol and store the information that fights make you uncomfortable and you can get rid of those uncomfortable feelings by using a little alcohol. So that information is stored about married life and alcohol, and over a period of time alcohol becomes their way of handling marital arguments.

There may be something about your job you don't like. It might be repetitious or noisy, but you can't quit because of economic circumstances. You may find that you can put in a good five days of work if you can look forward to a few beers on Friday evening. Your reward for sticking it out on that stinking job is a few beers. Using that as a reward relieves the tension of that job. Over a period of time, this becomes a regular routine. You can hardly wait to get off work on Friday so you can head for the bar, home, or wherever you do your drinking. Maybe instead of beer you try a little whiskey and really get yourself soused, but the tension is relieved. You really like that feeling and think you're entitled to it, so you may soon extend that to include Saturday and Sunday, too. Over a period of time, you may reach the point where you're really not in very good shape when Monday rolls around, but you realize you can't go in to work drunk so you quit. Monday you feel pretty rough, Tuesday a little better, and by Wednesday and Thursday you're in good shape again, but on Friday you're back into the cycle. You've learned how to handle job dissatisfaction with alcohol and stored that information in the brain.

You may have money problems. These money problems make you uncomfortable, but you know you can't get more money. You now need some relief from this worry and decide maybe you ought to have a couple beers and relax. Then you'll feel better about those money problems. After doing that a couple of times, you find, by God, it works. Of course, when the drinking is over those problems are still there, but you feel a little better while you're drinking. So you build up information in the subconscious that this is the way to handle money problems.

You may have driving problems. I always like to mention this, although you may wonder why: If you take a trip of a reasonable distance, for example, from Detroit to Montreal, you may find the drive a little boring. It's about a twelve-hour expressway drive, and there isn't too much to see. A stop now and then for gas or a bite to eat still equals a boring trip. However, you find that trip can be a little pleasanter if you turn on the stereo, open a bottle of beer, and sip on that. That seems to relax you and make you feel a little better. Since you make that trip every year, you may try a few shots of whiskey instead of beer. The trip becomes even more relaxing. That's the way to take a long-distance trip. Plenty of booze, the stereo humming, that makes a nice trip—like sitting in your living room having a few cocktails. I'll mention later another gentleman who had the same solution for driving to Florida.

Sex situations, for instance when young people don't know how to handle their sexual desires or male/female relationships, often fall into this alcohol-help category. I've run into the hypothetical case I'm talking about quite frequently: A young boy finds he's very uncomfortable and shy around girls. Because of his embarrassment, as a teenager he would cross to the other side of the street when he saw girls coming down his side of the street. However, he discovered that a little alcohol gave him some bravado and decided this was the way to handle that situation, i.e., if you're around females and want to converse or make sexual overtures, have something to drink. So he learned to cope with those emotions and stored that information as a teenager. As he grew older, this is the way he continued to approach it.

I refer to these sexual situations because they are common problems. One young man about thirty-five years old had done very well in the hospital recovery program. He'd been released and was returning as an out-patient. About two weeks later, for no apparent reason, he started to drink again, and in another week he was back in the hospital.

I talked to this fellow. I asked, "What's wrong? What happened? Don't you have any clues as to what's going on?"

"No, I just had to start drinking again."

"Well, okay if you don't know what it was," I said.

It happened again, three or four times. One day he attended this lecture. After the meeting, he came up to talk to me. There was no one else around and he said, "Don, I've been in and out of this hospital five times this year, and you know what it is, Don? It's sex."

I replied, "Is that your problem? Why didn't you tell somebody before?"

He said, "Well as a young boy I was afraid of girls. However, I found that if I had a few beers or shots, I became the life of the party. I really attracted women, and I carried this on into my married life. I can't have sex with my wife unless I have some booze. Otherwise, I'm afraid of her. I can do okay for about a week after I leave the hospital

55

because I'd avoid my wife in a sexual situation. Eventually sexual needs would arise and the only way I could cope with them was to have a drink."

This is what he'd learned, so that was his big problem now. He's not the only one with this problem. For both men and women tying alcohol and sex together is a common problem, because sex is a very strong desire in us. In fact, if anything could be instinctive with us, sex may be it. Now if you tie that to alcohol and don't do anything about it, I can guarantee you'll always go back to drinking. You have to do something about that. In many cases, alcohol tied with sex requires long, deep-seated therapy to root out that problem which inhibits or prevents you from becoming a sexually active person without alcohol.

Among the many other situations for which alcohol provides a solution is sports. You may find that to really enjoy a little sporting activity, be it softball, or whatever, it's always nice to have a case of beer handy. It seems to make the game more palatable. As a spectator at a game I'm sure you've seen people sloshing beer or whiskey down because they learned to do that over a period of time. The way to attend sporting events is to drink—this is the way to do it.

When you're young, being with your peers can be a problem, too. A group of girls get together for a little pajama party and they are busy talking about boys when someone suggests that they try something to drink. The parents aren't home, so they try some beer. It tastes rather strange, but they don't feel nervous about joining the conversation now. Everybody loosens up a little bit and acts a little funnier. The teenagers, as they grow older, have women friends, and when they go out, what do they do? Go to a bar or someone's house to have a few drinks while they're visiting. They learn to drink when they're among their peers.

I could go on and on, but you can see what's happening here. We've loaded our subconscious with information on everyday experiences tied to alcohol. Now perhaps you begin having problems with alcohol because you begin abusing alcohol. Realizing you're in a distressed state, you tell yourself, *I'm just not going to drink anymore.* Here you are, the typical person who started drinking as a teenager, now in your middle thirties or early forties with alcohol-related problems and telling yourself you aren't going to drink anymore.

If you were to tell me that, I'd tell you, "Well, I'll guarantee that you are."

You'd say, "No, I'm just not drinking anymore."

I'd have to disagree again. The only way you can learn to avoid drinking is to start doing something about it.

As an example, maybe one day you end up in jail. Now most of us don't spend much time in jail, so our brains don't have information on that. Perhaps you were out partying with the gang while the wife sat home and you ended up in jail for drunk driving. You go through the whole routine with the breathalizer and eventually end up in front of the judge. The judge says, "Well, I'll put you on a little probation here," et cetera. Eventually, you get out of jail. Standing in front of the courthouse, you say, "Oh, my God, that was a terrible experience. I never want to go through that again. It's a terrible, degrading experience. I'm never drinking again."

So you go home and whom do you meet? The wife. She says, "Where the hell have you been?"

You say, "Well, I've been in jail, dear."

Then the fight starts. "In jail?" she says. "I'll bet it's that lousy drinking of yours that got you in jail."

"What do you mean, my lousy drinking? You drink as much as me," and the old fight starts. And what are you conditioned to do when you fight with your wife? Get out and have a beer. That's the way you handle those fights. Don't let her yell at you that way. Get the hell out of the house and have a drink. You're programmed to do that.

Well, you get over that one, and one evening while you're sitting at home the phone rings. It's one of your buddies. "Don, I hear you've lost your license. That's a real bummer. A few of the guys are headed for Hines Park to throw Frisbees. Do you want to go with us?"

"Boy, hell yes, I'll go—but I can't drink. I'm not drinking."

"Well, that's okay; you don't have to drink. Just come along. You'll feel better if you get out of the house."

They break out a case of beer and everyone's running around throwing Frisbees. Everyone seems to be having a good time, between grabbing beer and Frisbees. However, your brain has been programmed that if you're playing a little Frisbee, you have some beer with it. That's the way it's done, and soon you begin to feel uncomfortable about the whole thing. You say, "Gee, I don't know what the hell is wrong with me, but I just don't feel right. I don't enjoy this, and I used to like coming over here with the boys to throw the Frisbee around." Your brain is saying, *Look, dummy, get a beer*. Those pressures are almost insurmountable. You can't fight them off because you're programmed to follow them.

You've learned how to throw Frisbees at Hines Park—you have beer when you throw Frisbees.

Maybe you're like this sixty-year-old guy who drove to Florida every year. He was progressing very well in the alcohol recovery program and one day told the therapist he and his wife were going to Florida.

The therapist said, "Well, have a good time. You know you've been working hard at this recovery, so you'd better not drink."

"Heck, hey, I know that. I ain't gonna drink. That's the last thing I'd do. I'm really feeling good now."

But the next time the therapist saw him was in the emergency room of the hospital. The therapist asked. "What happened? What happened to you? I saw you only three days ago, and you said you'll never drink again. What happened to your Florida trip?"

"I don't know. I don't know what happened. All I know is I began to feel uncomfortable about the trip and I had been really looking forward to it. I just didn't feel right, but I didn't know what it was. I started thinking that it was a long way to drive to Florida. Then I thought, *Well, gee whiz, you've been driving there for twenty years, and the way to make it a little easier is to have some booze.* I figured that I couldn't let my wife know I was drinking again. I had to be clever about this: *Maybe what I'll do is fill the windshield washer bag with booze, drill a little hole through the firewall of the car, and run the hose underneath the dashboard. I'll tell the wife we have to drive at night because traffic isn't so heavy. When she isn't looking, I'll just grab that hose, stick it in my mouth, press the windshield washer button, and get a shot of booze.* So the man tried that, but he was already sick from alcoholism so it took only a little booze before he was sick again in a hospital halfway to Florida. This actually happened. He had learned that you use booze to drive to Florida.

RE-LEARNING LIFE WITHOUT ALCOHOL

So you've decided to quit drinking, you're out of the hospital, and now you're going to a party. About an hour or two before it's time to go, you begin to get a little sweaty. You don't understand why, but you don't feel right. You're feeling uncomfortable about the party because you've been going to parties for twenty years and getting soused. I guarantee that when you go to that party sober you won't enjoy it a bit.

58

You won't know what to do with yourself, because you have to have alcohol at a party. You've learned this. Let's refer to that formula we began with to see what you must do. You have to learn how to go to parties without alcohol. Motivation is there. You don't want to drink. How can you learn to go to parties without drinking? The answer is you have to experience it. This is Step 2 or Hands-On. You have to go to parties, and you have to tough it through without alcohol. The first party without alcohol may be a miserable experience. You don't know whom to talk to, everybody is telling the same jokes, and you think everyone is drinking except you. You don't feel right. Well, if you're that uncomfortable leave, but you'll have to go back and do it again. Don't avoid parties completely. Gradually you'll build up information in the brain about parties without alcohol and find that some of those are good experiences. You have to re-learn. The reward, of course, is any of the rewards for staying away from alcohol. You may decide that the party was terrible, but the next day you feel good. You don't have a hangover, and that's a good deal. You had a lousy time last night, but you feel good now and that's the reward. In order to be able to cope with parties again, you keep repeating those experiences without alcohol.

The same is true for all of those alcohol-related solutions. Within your marriage, instead of going for the bottle when you're arguing with the wife, take a walk around the block. Tell her you don't want to argue anymore. If she's persistent, leave the house, but try to work this thing out without alcohol.

The same thing applies to job problems. If you're a woman with a job that tells you every Friday to go out and get drunk, find something else to do. Take up tennis, golf, bowling, reading, or anything that interests you. Learn to handle that Friday night situation without alcohol. You'll be uncomfortable at first, but the more you do it the more experience you build up.

The reason why we see forty-year-old long-term drinkers with the personalities of young teenagers is the inability to cope with problems. People who learned to handle their problems with alcohol as young teenagers still can't handle them forty-five years later. The mind is very flexible, so you can re-learn rapidly, whether the problem is marital, peers, sex, money, your job, or driving. You won't enjoy it the first few times, but gradually you'll build up information in the subconscious which will help you along. Peer pressure is prevalent in many of these situations. The men say, "Well, when I go with the boys to the bowling alley everyone is drinking." Or the gals say, "Any time we get together for

club night, you have to have a few cocktails because the other gals do.''
You don't. You don't need it, and you'll find that everybody doesn't do
it—or at least they don't all abuse alcohol. The upshot of the whole thing
is: You re-learn. You won't accomplish this in a day or a week and it
may take a year, but it can be done.

There is one ever-present danger, intermittent though it may be, for
which I want to prepare you. You may have something isolated in your
brain which doesn't occur all the time. Maybe you went to Alaska once
hunting and partying with some guys and gals about fifteen years ago.
Everybody got drunk; at least you thought so. You certainly tried hard
enough and got really snorkled. Well, you haven't been drinking for
about ten years and the wife says, ''Let's go to Alaska like we did fifteen
years ago.'' You're all primed to go, only this time you aren't drinking.
A couple of days before leaving, you begin to get messages you don't
understand: *My God, I just don't feel right. I'm uptight about this hunting
trip.* Of course you are, because our subconscious is telling you, *Look,
information in your brain on hunting trips to Alaska says to get drunk.
That's the way to go to Alaska.* It's an experience you haven't re-learned
since you stopped drinking. That's the ever-present danger and one of
the principal reasons why we see longtime recovering alcoholics suddenly
go back to drinking for no apparent reason. They've encountered a situation which they haven't re-learned yet. The subconscious has told them
to drink.

To sum this all up: Like anything else, we learn to drink. Once we
learn it, we really learn it. We tend to remember those drinking situations,
and we generally emphasize the good parts and forget the bad parts. If
we didn't, we'd probably all go crazy. We're programmed for everything
we do, and we're certainly programmed in our drinking. In a nutshell,
alcoholics have to go about their business as alcoholics or recovering
alcoholics by becoming involved in a whole spectrum of social activities
without alcohol. They're not cripples. Alcoholics should participate in
many activities so they can re-learn how to do things without alcohol.
Only after doing that will they be well on the way to recovery.

Talk 5

Alcoholic or Problem Drinker?

ALCOHOLIC

Psychological
problems

Physiological
problems

Psychological
addiction

PROBLEM DRINKER

Psychological
problems

Physiological
problems

Psychological
addiction

PHYSIOLOGICAL ADDICTION

Alcoholic has this.

Problem drinker does not.

. . . THEREFORE . . .
alcoholic has physical factor motivation.

Problem drinker does not.

Alcoholic wants to be a problem drinker
so he can have alcohol.

CAUSE?

Probably body chemistry.

. . . BUT . . .
knowledge of cause will probably not
allow a return to alcohol.

This talk will discuss why some people are alcoholics or problem drinkers. This worries many people, because they hope they're problem drinkers instead of alcoholics, so they won't have to give up alcohol.

DIFFERENCES

What differentiates the alcoholic from the problem drinker? Well, one way of looking at it is that the problem drinker becomes psychologically addicted to alcohol. He needs alcohol to handle his psychological, emotional make-up; it's a behavioral problem. However, in addition to this psychological problem, the alcoholic has a physical need for alcohol. He develops a physical addiction. This physical addiction is the thing which differentiates the alcoholic from the problem drinker. Most alcoholics can recall the time when they seemed to trigger the physical need or addiction and from that point in their lives they could never drink in the old way. It is for these reasons—this combination of both psychological and physiological addiction—that alcoholism is truly a disease.

MOTIVATION

If we look at motivation, the problem drinker is generally motivated temporarily to do something about his drinking because of some problem he's having, for example, drunk driving or an assault on someone which relates directly to alcohol. He may do something about his drinking, but usually he is not sufficiently motivated to make a change over a long period of time. On the other hand, the alcoholic has no choice. The physical addiction to alcohol, once those symptoms are triggered and continued, can only lead to death. That's the end result of continued drinking for the alcoholic, because the body chemistry, the mind, the person's ability to cope with alcohol are completely lost, and alcohol wins out. Alcohol is a tremendous killer. It's no longer only a poison to the alcoholic. Alcohol means death to the alcoholic.

Generally, before it kills the alcoholic, alcohol ruins many, many areas of his life. It can ruin his family life, his self-respect, his job, and so on. (Very few literally end up on skid row, but they deteriorate as far as life itself is concerned. As we think of it, skid row is an unpleasant problem in a distant place for people we don't know. The alcoholic, unfortunately, becomes one of those persons living on skid row.) The alcoholic recognizes some of this and will be motivated by the knowledge that this physical need is killing him. That physical need can turn itself around to some type of motivation.

WHY ME?

It's said now that people who are alcoholics are probably born that way. Why we don't seem to know. Are there many alcoholics who have never had a drink? Is it possible that they don't suffer from the disease alcoholism simply because they don't drink and never trigger the symptoms? It is. As we pointed out, alcoholism is a progressive disease. If an alcoholic quits drinking, the disease is temporarily arrested, but it is never cured. If that person goes back to drinking alcohol, then the effect of alcohol on him is more devastating than it ever was. This is even true of people who have given up alcohol for long periods of time (twenty to twenty-five years). If they return to drinking, they will experience the severe symptoms of alcoholism as more pronounced than ever before. We don't know why people are alcoholics. This has been called the mystery of alcoholism. We know that for some people food, plus a faulty pancreas over a period of time, results in diabetes. It seems that for some people, alcohol plus a faulty we-don't-know-what over a period of time results in alcoholism.

COMPARISON WITH DIABETES

It was found in 1929 that diabetes, plus perhaps insulin or an oral medication, a controlled diet, and some type of therapy, would lead to a somewhat healthy person, i.e., a person with the ability to live. Prior to 1929, a diagnosis of diabetes was tantamount to a death sentence. The alcoholic's return to drinking parallels the case of the diabetic who doesn't stick strictly to a regimen. In both cases, the symptoms of the disease are triggered again, resulting in severe illness or death from their disease.

CAUSE OF ALCOHOLISM

Some people have thought the unknown or mystery factor in the alcoholic might be an allergy factor, while others thought it was a matter of genetics, a metabolic problem, or hypoglycemia, because hypoglycemics do quite well temporarily on alcohol. (It relieves their symptoms.) Some people thought it was a willpower problem. Well, willpower doesn't do much for alcohol. A good test of willpower is to try to suppress a sneeze. That's willpower. You won't make it and this parallels willpower with alcohol. Some people still believe that it is a purely psychological behavior pattern. Many psychologists say that an alcoholic is a person who has developed psychological dependence. From our experience in talking with alcoholics, we've concluded that the problem is much more complicated. There are unknown physical factors involved. Regarding intelligence, the observation I can make is that practically all of the alcoholics I've had experience with are fairly intelligent. Many, many people think that alcoholism is a moral problem, i.e., a moral conflict within the person. Some people think it's only a personality cover-up or a way of dealing with life's problems. Others think it's strictly an emotional disease where some people can't compete emotionally with their problems so they use alcohol. Nobody really knows what the unknown or so-called X factor is. Maybe, it's a combination of these ideas, plus a few more. We do know that the alcoholic, as opposed to the problem drinker, can't continue to drink, because that leads to insanity and/or death. The only thing the alcoholic can do is eventually accept the fact that he has this disease and do something about it. Also, problem drinkers through education, learning about alcohol, and recognizing that they have a problem and alcohol is not the magic elixir or substance they think it is, can be motivated to do something to control their drinking. Hopefully, they will.

FURTHER COMPARISON BETWEEN ALCOHOLICS AND PROBLEM DRINKERS

I hope I've been able to get across the point that the alcoholic is in a physically diseased state and for some reason has a predisposition to physical deterioration with alcohol. The problem drinker doesn't have the physical need but does have the psychological need.

Similarly, the severe problem drinker has as much sociological damage as the alcoholic. People who develop true symptoms of alcoholism usually pass through an addictive pattern stage. Both alcoholics and problem drinkers start at the solution stage—to drink to change the way they feel. Both pass into the problem stage and then enter the resistance stage, where they will resist any suggestion that they have a problem with alcohol. Most problem drinkers remain in the resistance stage and are able to continue drinking throughout their lives. The alcoholic goes beyond that stage into what we call a *resigned* stage. At the resigned stage, the person recognizes physical dependency and addiction, becomes somewhat resigned to this fate, and, in most cases, continues drinking. Part of this is because he is not aware that help is available or that there are alternatives. The alcoholic then passes into the helpless stage. He can't help himself and other people can't help him, so he dies.

RECOVERY PROSPECTS

I can only continue to stress the fact that modern-day treatment of alcoholism says that people who are alcoholics cannot drink. If they stop drinking, the symptoms will remain dormant. It's been said that this is the only true physical disease which has a good prognosis for recovery, because most other afflictions require continuing treatment and have a limited prospect for recovery. Alcoholism is a major disease which has a good prospect for recovery.

IDENTIFICATION OF ALCOHOLISM

Psychologists or psychotherapists who tell alcoholics that alcoholism is not a true disease state are wrong. They don't know the trigger mechanism of alcoholism and have little, if any, understanding of the true physical addiction of alcohol. Many are not trained as medical doctors. Even then, in many of our medical schools older doctors learned little, if any, comprehension of alcoholism. This contributes to the confusion people have identifying themselves as alcoholics or problem drinkers. It really doesn't matter because the recovery for both groups is similar—they should both stay away from alcohol. The alcoholic hopes he is a problem drinker so that he can go back to alcohol, and the problem drinker justifies his continued drinking by saying he's not an alcoholic. I suggest to alcoholics that they not rely on thinking of themselves as problem drinkers, because then they are usually hospitalized and then return to drinking several times over before they finally give up alcohol. It's a trap, a vicious circle. Try to help yourself by identifying yourself as an alcoholic or problem drinker, but remember that neither is a healthy person. The purpose of this book and these talks is to do something about alcohol when we use it in a problem setting instead of a social setting.

PUBLIC ATTITUDE

Neither the alcoholic nor problem drinker should worry about people who have no understanding of what they're up against. Every now and then you'll read a newspaper article suggesting that the tax on liquor sales should be used to set up alcoholic rehabilitation centers. People vote against it in an attitude of "Let the lousy drunks help themselves." This indicates a misunderstanding on the part of the public. Dr. Jelnick, one of the early pioneers in studying alcoholism as a disease, once said, "One will not understand alcohol as a problem until he sees it as a solution." Those people who are alcoholics or problem drinkers know very well that alcohol is not a viable solution to any problem.

Talk 6

Time and Recovery

Since the beginning of these talks, we've covered topics such as mood-altering drugs. The purpose there, of course, was to acquaint you with alcohol and classify it. Then we had a talk on what alcohol is, followed by talks on physical damage from alcohol and alcohol as learned behavior. Our last talk was on the alcoholic and problem drinker. These talks were designed to get people to recognize the extent of their drinking problems, because there is a strong tendency not to. It's commonly called *denial*. I talked about that before, mentioning that in many cases people are unaware of this denial. Really, if you're honest with yourself and you have a drinking problem, you should be motivated to do something about it. Now the problem becomes: What are you going to do about this drinking problem? That's what I'd like to talk about next.

This talk is called "Time and Recovery" because I've found that many alcohol abuse treatment programs really don't stress the recovery aspect—what a person has to do to achieve recovery and how much time is involved. Other programs seem to dwell on helping people identify with being alcoholics. These people get into therapy, but they don't have a plan, which I think they should have. It's the absence of this plan and the absence of any idea of how much time is involved and what their condition in common medical terms should be over a period of time that lead many people back to drink. Either because they feel they've failed in their attempt to stay away from alcohol or have succeeded and are perfectly well, they think they can go back to drinking. So that's the essence of this talk on time and recovery.

This talk is designed to take the case of a person who has been drinking for a period of time and is hospitalized for alcoholism. I think we can consider this our most severe case of alcoholism. Those of you in the audience who haven't gone that far in your drinking can still see, as you follow the talk, where you would come into the recovery program.

DRINKING YEARS

For the typical alcoholic, alcoholism begins with what we'll call *the drinking years*. Any alcoholic you talk to, if you talk to him long enough,

71

will start to give you some information about his drinking experiences. Most alcoholics will tell you that drinking was a good experience to begin with, but then they seemed to enter a period of physical and mental degradation or deterioration. In other words, alcohol caused them to look lousy and feel lousy mentally.

LINE OF ALCOHOLISM

Most alcoholics, then, seem to recall a period when for some reason they crossed the line into alcoholism. The symptoms of alcoholism were triggered, such as the shaking experiences and the hangovers which last two or three days, instead of twenty-four hours. They find that the only relief they can get (if they don't wait out those two or three days) is to have another drink. And, of course, this drinking time gets longer and longer. Many people can recall the time when they seemed to get into that type of effect—when those symptoms of alcoholism were really triggered. It's like an invisible line, and we'll call that the *line of alcoholism*. The line is very important. If you reach the point where you trigger the extreme symptoms of alcoholism and continue to drink, you'll die.

TERMINAL

If we think in terms commonly used to identify patients in a hospital setting, your condition would be called *terminal* when you cross the line of alcoholism. We hear much about terminal cancer patients. Well, here we have the terminal alcoholic. The prognosis is that if you keep drinking and you're an alcoholic, you'll die of alcoholism. We're not saying that as soon as you trigger the symptoms of alcoholism you'll drop dead. No, it will take time and cause much destruction in your life before it kills you. However, your condition in a medical sense is terminal. Eventually alcoholics reach a point where what we call *non-drinking* begins. For some, this will occur because death occurs. Their terminal condition leads to death. Any of us who have worked in this field know they die. They die of the ravages of the disease alcoholism. For those people, time as we know it ends.

RECOVERY BEGINS

However, some people stop drinking because they end up in a hospital and cross the non-drinking line. In many cases, they're very close to death but don't realize it. As I mentioned before, one out of twenty alcoholics die in the hospital while withdrawing from alcohol. However, when they cross the non-drinking line they're on the way to recovery. The time involved in recovery is part of what we'll talk about now.

Typically, alcoholics enter the hospital as they cross the non-drinking line and they're in very poor condition. Many of them enter the hospital in a very jovial mood because they're drugged with alcohol. However, we know from past experiences what kind of shape these people will be in when the alcohol wears off. In fact, some people come to the hospital drunk or intoxicated because they're afraid to get there any other way. They're afraid they'll go into the DTs or something, and they're in sad shape.

INTENSIVE CARE (FIRST FIFTEEN DAYS)

When they enter a hospital suffering from acute and chronic alcoholism, they're in what we call an intensive-care situation which is every bit as intensive as that of a person entering a hospital with a heart attack. You won't see cardiac monitors on them or doctors and nurses running around, but they're extremely ill and the medical staff knows this. This condition generally lasts from a week to fifteen days. During the first fifteen days of the recovery period, they're in an intensive-care situation and need medical help. They need medical help to prevent a central nervous system collapse, cardiac arrest, or some other problem. The medical care generally includes some type of sedative as a substitute for alcohol. In some of the earlier treatment programs, patients were given small amounts of alcohol in gradually decreasing dosages. Now, we substitute drugs, such as Librium or Valium, which are rather strong tranquillizers but not nearly as strong as alcohol. If you talk to people in that hospital setting, they'll tell you this stuff doesn't compare at all with alcohol. "I want some alcohol," is reiterated. That's how bad they feel. Also, in that hospital setting you can receive what we call *psycho-*

73

logical help. This help can take many forms, but it's not any type of deep therapy. These are supportive talks with a therapist, a doctor, or another member of the medical staff. He will try to get you in a proper frame of mind for recovery by explaining to you your condition and what can be done about it. Most hospital treatment programs begin to give you some information on alcoholism at this point. The information usually consists of instructive lectures (similar to the first five talks I've given here) to explain the causes of alcoholism. Often people are so sick they don't grasp much of this. If you're half dead, as we mentioned, the staff really doesn't expect you to remember very well. However, this is a good point (because the person is very ill) to try to get some of these thoughts into the conscious part of the brain. Hopefully, some of these ideas will shift into the subconscious and get the person's mind working on something besides physical ills.

The Urge to Drink

Just because they enter a hospital, people don't lose the desire to drink. An "urge" means a compulsion to drink, and we call it *addiction*. Addiction is need—the need to drink. If you're an alcoholic, you need to drink. As we said before, it's not a willpower game. It's a need. What we have to do is substitute other things for that need. This urge to drink can be a high or low urge.

As you start out in the hospital you're very ill, so most likely you won't want anything to drink. People say, "I'm in the hospital now—good. Maybe they'll give me something so I can stay away from that alcohol." So for approximately the first couple of days people don't want any alcohol. As I said, however, tranquillizers don't work very well. They're not as strong as alcohol, so the urge to drink starts building. That urge continues to build from a low to a relatively high urge in the hospital setting. What they're doing in the intensive-care setting is detoxing you or getting your body physically away from alcohol. But believe me, it doesn't get your mind away from alcohol. Detoxifying the body doesn't detoxify the mind. Your mind is still possessed with that need for alcohol. At the end of this detoxification or intensive-care period (say at the end of fifteen days), many people are liable to walk out of the hospital without medical permission. If so, the first thing they do is get a drink. Even if you leave the hospital after a week or two with medical permission, you'll probably have a very strong urge to drink. We call this a *flare-up* or *dry drunk*. During the intensive care program, those flare-ups will be minor in nature and increase in intensity. Consequently, you're apt to have a very strong flare-up on the day you leave the hospital. A flare-up will cause you to return to drinking. We're telling you this now so you can be alert for that type of reaction. Even though they don't drink at this point, some people will have all the symptoms of drinking. Though they haven't touched any alcohol, they even experience the hangover. This is called a *dry drunk*; that's how flare-ups work in the recovery process. Be prepared with a plan to combat flare-ups. The plan may involve using Antabuse temporarily or contacting an A.A. friend or going to the hospital for help. Just be prepared, because the urge to drink will occur.

CRITICAL (UP TO ONE MONTH)

Being out of the hospital doesn't mean that you're no longer ill. Your condition has changed from an intensive-care situation to what we call *critical*. Medically, you're critical. People may wonder why they're not in the hospital if their condition is critical. For instance, if you were a Catholic priest suffering from alcoholism in the Detroit area, you would still be out at a convalescent center. They recognize how critical the condition is. It's also recognized in the hospital setting, but we realize that treatment of alcoholism cannot be confined to the hospital. Part of the recovery is getting people out, but don't let that deceive you. Your condition is medically critical, and the condition will last about one month. During that period you have to do things to effect your recovery, and we suggest that you continue with medical help. Many people who begin recovery without being hospitalized begin in the critical stage. Don't let the absence of being in a hospital fool you.

Medical Help

Now let's talk a little about medical help, because you will have physical complaints. They may be major or minor, and many may be

75

psychosomatic in origin, i.e., you may feel headachy or have a growling stomach, cramps, or intestinal pains and those symptoms are real. As an example, ulcers are caused by psychosomatic conditions. However, if you're bleeding in the stomach, then you know it's real. (You even bleed to death from a stomach ulcer.) The same is true in alcoholism. Those headaches, minor aches and pains and feelings of uneasiness are real so you should see a doctor. Some people think they can't afford a doctor. The hell you can't. You can afford to buy the booze when you're drinking, so now you can afford a little money to visit the doctor. If you haven't any money, medical programs which will allow you to see a doctor are available. Some people say, "I'm ashamed to go to the doctor." My response to that is: "What the hell is there to be ashamed about when you're fighting for your life? You're in a death situation here. It's hardly rational to be ashamed when you're fighting for your life." You must go out and work with a doctor on these complaints. In some cases, the doctor may say he can't find anything seriously wrong but may prescribe aspirin, a painkiller, or Maalox or just give you a good talking to. One thing he won't do is throw you out of the office. Many people get relief from telling someone about their medical complaints. I suggest you do that. If you don't, you'll use those physical complaints to justify drinking. You might say something like, "If a nice person like me has this lousy stomach or headache, I'm entitled to a drink." You'll talk yourself into it, so don't allow yourself that excuse. Get medical help.

Also, you may find that some of these complaints aren't very minor. Some people have severe liver damage, heart muscle damage, gastritis, an altered metabolism, or similar ailments. All of these things can be worked out with a medical doctor. If you don't work these complaints out, once again, the complaints will lead you right back to drinking.

Another thing in this area you can begin thinking about is nutrition. Think about the good things you can put into your body instead of the poison alcohol. Maybe you want to go on a megavitamin kick. It won't hurt you and may do you some good, because you should be eating a well-balanced diet. If your metabolism isn't quite right and you're working with a doctor, he will advise you which foods to avoid. You should be very conscious of the things you're putting into your body. If you're an alcoholic who has been drinking for a period of time, you have liver damage. Everybody who drinks heavily does. If it's just a case of a fatty liver, a good, balanced diet will cause it to rejuvenate itself. As the liver rejuvenates or heals itself, you'll feel better.

Psychological Help (and/or Group Therapy)

Also, you should be working in the psychological area. This can use some defining because *psychological* can mean several things. It could mean working with a psychiatrist, a psychologist, or a therapist or working in a group-therapy setting. To begin with, the one thing I recommend is work in a group-therapy situation, with directed therapy. In directed therapy, the group leader is a trained counselor. Don't be ashamed of that; you don't beat alcoholism on your own. You need help. Some people can gain this therapy at Alcoholics Anonymous meetings (see Talk 8) if they're working with a good sponsor. Usually, you don't have directed therapy at A.A. meetings. It depends on the specific group. However, if that's your preference, go to A.A. Some people have severe psychological (mental) problems. By that we don't mean that they are insane, "out of their gourd," or "gone bananas," but they have things on their minds which aren't working out quite right. They don't have the right answers and are going about the solutions wrong. If it's an immediate or crisis-like problem (family-type thing), perhaps a psychologist can help immediately. Psychologists put out brush fires. However, if your problems are more deep-seated, perhaps you need the help of a psychiatrist. A psychiatrist differs from a psychologist in that he has a medical background. I like to explain this to people because if they decide to work with a psychiatrist, they should expect to make a commitment of at least one year. It takes that long to get any effect from a psychiatrist in most cases. Also, on the subject of doctors, shop around. If you're working with someone but not getting results (remember, you're battling for your life), shop around until you find someone you think is doing you some good. It's your choice.

Information

For a one-month period you should be getting information about alcoholism. You should attend lectures and, if you like to read, read about alcoholism. Get all the information available. The reason for this is that we begin to treat alcoholism as a person—yes, alcohol as a person. When you treat alcohol as a person, you become afraid and fearful of the thing which is causing you all this distress. Then that fear of alcohol can drive you back to drinking. You'll throw in the towel, saying, "The heck

77

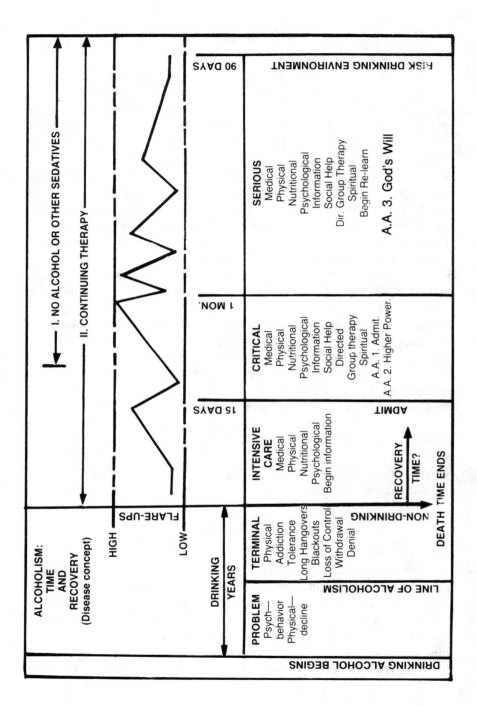

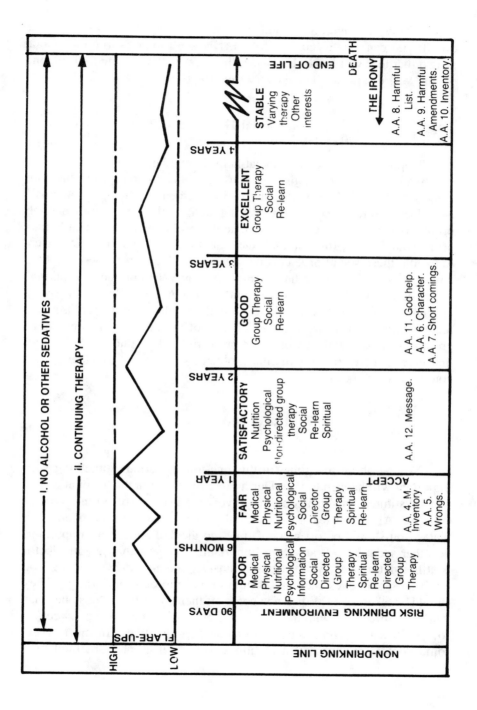

with it—my old friend has won." One way to get around this is to find out all you can about your old friend. Know all there is to know about it, and that fear will leave. Likewise, the chance of returning to drink out of fear will disappear. This is very important.

Social Help

People now should seek social help. Social help ties in a little with working with a psychologist, or you can think of it as working with someone who can help with your social problems. "Social problems" here doesn't refer to how you're getting along with society. It means job problems if you've lost your job or family problems if there is a break-up in your family, for example. Get some professional help. Don't try to handle these social problems on your own. The help is there, so take advantage of it. If you're having problems on your job due to drinking, it can be arranged for you to talk with your employer about a recovery program. In most cases, employers are extremely helpful, because they recognize alcoholism as a disease. Many of the larger companies have groups or departments to work with problem drinkers and alcoholics. So that help is there. If it's a marital problem, you can get together with a counselor to work on it.

Use of Sedatives

Now at about this time (in this one-month period) something very important will happen to you. During intensive care in the hospital, drugs wre substituted for the alcohol to prevent the DTs or some other type of collapse. After you leave the hospital, prior to reaching the one-month mark, you should be off alcohol, i.e., no alcohol and, more important, no other sedatives. That's very important. I suggest that if your doctor is still sedating you, you seriously consider seeing another doctor. You don't need sedatives such as Librium or Valium or similar drugs. They should be taken away. When you come off them, you'll feel lousy because you'll go through a withdrawal period, but stick it out. After a week or so, you'll start feeling better—no alcohol or sedatives. In most cases, some doctors recommend a nighttime aid, such as phenobarbital or a sleeping aid called Dalmane, a non-barbiturate type of sleep preparation. That may be helpful, but these are the only sedatives I recommend, if necessary. I advise, too, if you're nervous and irritable and can't sleep you have some relief during the evening. Some doctors don't agree—however, I think being rested is invaluable at this point in order to carry out your therapy.

END OF MONTH

You're in what we call a *therapy setting* now at the end of one month's recovery. Regarding the flare-ups, a high urge to drink may affect you a few days after you come out of the hospital. However, you'll come down to a very low level where you won't even feel like drinking. You simply won't have that urge. Alcoholism or any type of addiction is easy to handle when the urge is low. It's no problem. Why would it be a problem if you don't have the urge to drink? However, what happens to you and most people is that in the one-month period the low urge for drink will gradually become extremely high, until at the end of the month you're in extreme danger of drinking. Usually people feel great as they near the end of a month: "I've gone a whole month without alcohol. I feel great." Most people have not accomplished that in many a year. They begin to feel so great that the feelings of happiness and greatness they're experiencing begin to make them nervous. It's a high, a natural high, but recovering alcoholics don't know how to cope with these feelings. They begin to get upset about the nervousness they're feeling because they're feeling so good. What does that lead to? The mind's old way of handling that nervousness—*get a drink, get a drink*. If you're not careful, you'll return to drinking because you feel so good. Don't deceive yourself; you're still very ill. You're critically ill.

SERIOUS (UP TO NINETY DAYS)

At the end of a month and up to ninety days, we can think of your medical condition as progressing from critical to serious. Some time has elapsed, but you're still serious. Something is happening with those flare-ups during that ninety-day period. In most cases, that high at thirty days will decline. This will be followed with high urges, low urges, and high and low periodic flare-ups. They become less and less intense and further apart as time without alcohol increases. This is very important to know, because some people have the flare-ups weekly during this period. One week they'll have no desire at all to drink, but in a week or two they may feel they have to have a drink. Some people feel so disoriented that they think they have the flu. They'll even have all the symptoms, except there won't be any temperature. These are some of the vague medical complaints we've discussed. This is the body's need for alcohol expressing itself. Your body is saying, *I've got to have that alcohol,* but then soon it seems to say, *Well, I'm not getting it. I might as well give up on that.* Then you'll feel good for a week, until the body decides, *I want to try getting that stuff again.* That's a good way to look at it because you have to be on guard. I've talked to many people who say this is the first time anyone ever told them that would happen. They will add, "When I think about it, though, that's what happened the last time I quit drinking. I felt that I had to have a drink, and that feeling wouldn't go away. I didn't know what it was." At the end of ninety days, that urge will drop off if you're getting medical help and working with your nutrition, your medical complaints, and your psychologist, if you're seeing one. (You'd still be working with a psychologist up to ninety days and certainly still be seeing a psychiatrist.) Directed group therapy is also a necessity, but work with someone who knows his business. Surprisingly, many people with enormously important jobs, such as vice presidents of companies, et cetera, can't make decisions about their own personal lives when they're recovering from alcoholism. They have to be told. If you're working with a therapist who is trained in it, he can tell you exactly what you should do day by day. That's the kind of help you need, because you're not qualified to make those decisions. A.A. can help you here. Find someone in A.A. who has given you good advice and stick to him. If you're getting rotten advice, dump it and that person. Start making the decisions about where to get help.

Re-learning Process

Now up to here we still thnk you need some information on alcohol and some social help. *Social help* in this context has a somewhat different meaning. It might be referred to as your *social setting.* In order to acclimate yourself to a social atmosphere, you must begin with a re-learning process. Remember the talk we had on learning? After a one-month period, you should be working on re-learning your life—which means you should get out and do things. The only thing you shouldn't do in that first ninety days is risk a drinking environment. Stay away from drinking situations, such as parties, bars, or anyplace people are drinking. Even if you're a bar owner whose employees are dipping into the till, stay away from that bar. Find someone you trust to run it until you're back on your feet. Do not risk drinking situations. Other social areas get a green light. Even though you may not like it, go for a picnic with your wife and kids. If you're a mother, invite your husband and kids to go window-shopping or something. If you're used to drinking in these situations, you may be extremely uncomfortable, but you've got to start someplace. Make up your mind you're going to do it and do it. If you become uncomfortable or shaky at the picnic, tell your spouse you have to go home. If he is understanding, he'll go home with you so you'll be more comfortable. Hopefully, he'll realize you're still in serious condition. He would be sympathetic if you were in the hospital with an ulcerated colon, for example, and you're every bit as seriously ill as that person lying in a hospital.

Admit to Alcoholism

This takes you up to the ninety-day period. In the early stages of recovery, admit to your alcoholism because it is pretty obvious, but you don't have to accept the fact that you can't have alcohol anymore. This is pretty difficult, so don't drink, but leave the idea of acceptance until you have about a year of recovery in hand. Now let's see how far we're going with this thing. People tell me, "Now wait a minute, ninety days? Are you telling me that after ninety days I won't be in top shape?" Well, that's exactly what I'm telling you. No matter how you feel, you're still seriously ill. You have to put in some time yet. If you've been drinking for twenty years and have triggered the symptoms of alcoholism for twenty years and continued drinking, you won't recover from that illness in ninety days. Use your head; how could you possibly? We'll go on to the next stage now and see where we go with this thing, picking it up at the ninety-day point.

POOR (UP TO SIX MONTHS)

We still have to continue our recovery program. For the next six months we are in what can be described as a *poor* condition. It may seem that I'm repeating many of these things, but we still need help during this period for the same reasons previously discussed. Your social life in this period can include being involved in other people's drinking situations. After ninety days, there is nothing you as an alcoholic can't do that other people do except drink alcohol. Don't let anyone tell you that you're restricted to non-drinking situations, because you aren't. As you know, our way of life includes alcohol for most people. You'll be involved with people who are drinking, and there is no reason you can't be.

Every now and then, we have a person in here who is in softball or some other group activity. He says, "After the game everybody goes to the bar. How can I do that?"

I reply, "Why can't you do that? You just go over there with the rest but you don't drink any beer. Order a pop or coffee, or don't drink anything at all. If people ask what's wrong with you, chances are they have a drinking problem. People without drinking problems generally don't give a damn what other people are drinking, but those with drinking problems are aware of what other people are drinking. If someone asks, you don't have to say, 'It's none of your damn business.' Nor do you want to reply that you're an alcoholic, because they won't know what you're talking about—they'll think you're a damn drunk. Just tell them you have a bad stomach and the doctor said no more alcohol for a while. Give them some excuse, but don't drink. If you're very uncomfortable, and you probably will be, then leave. Say your good-byes, get up, and leave, but don't avoid going back to that situation next week. Go back to it. Start re-learning. Learn how to get along socially with people—both in drinking and non-drinking situations. You have to learn."

FAIR (UP TO ONE YEAR)

Now we also mention this six-month point in recovery because, as a rule, people come off that low at ninety days feeling like not drinking. However, that urge will build up gradually with some flare-ups here and there to a high at the end of six months—the urge to drink re-surfaces.

84

But if you stay away from alcohol, at that point your condition will progress to what we call *fair*. It will take you one year. What is the significance of that? Well, it means that most people can now accept life without alcohol. Acceptance is a crisis point in recovery because it finally cuts you off from alcohol, as compared to the admittance which occurred at one month, which still allowed you to think of alcohol as a final solution if all else failed.

SATISFACTORY (UP TO TWO YEARS)

After one year of treatment, your condition is satisfactory. Remember, when you are hospitalized for most ailments the doctor doesn't recommend your release from the hospital until your condition is satisfactory. By comparison, in recovering from alcoholism at the point where you haven't seen the inside of a hospital as an in-patient for over eleven months you have only now reached the satisfactory stage. Unfortunately, we don't treat alcoholism that way. When you see people who have been in the hospital with pneumonia, for example, they're pretty shaky when they first step out. They don't feel they're about to lick the world. That's how weak and shaky you are with your disease, alcoholism. Regardless of how well you think you are, you aren't.

The first time I gave this lecture (about four years ago) I told this to a gal who is a therapist now. She got so angry at me that she started calling me names. She was in the audience and said, "What the hell do you know about it? Damn it, I haven't had a drink in a year and I'm in great shape." She's a good friend of mine now and often mentions to me, "Don, that talk is just great. You were right and I was wrong. I thought I was in excellent shape at the end of a year, but I wasn't. I realize it now." This is many years later. Even after a year, a lot of denial was still in her head. So you should continue with your medical help, except you may no longer require a psychologist if you were seeing one. If you're seeing a psychiatrist, continue this treatment. At the end of the year you may have a tremendous flare-up. Feeling good a week before this, you're probably thinking, *I've got this licked now.* But for some reason many people (frequently therapists) return to drinking at that one-year point. One of the reasons for that might be because we're very anniversary-conscious. This point is like a birthday. It's one year now, and so you begin to take inventory. (That inventory is mentioned in one of the A.A. steps covered in Talk 8.) The way we take inventory presents us with two problems. You say, "Wow, look at what I've accomplished. I know all about alcohol and haven't had a drink in one year." As you begin to tell yourself what a big hero you are, you get the same feeling you got at the thirty-day point. You may have to go back to drinking to handle that feeling; it'll overwhelm you. That may sound strange to you, but I've seen it happen time and again. The other problem occurs when you realize you've been sober for a year but still feel like hell. You might say, "My job's screwed up and my marriage, too. Nothing's happened." Well, maybe the reason nothing has happened is because you haven't been working at these other things. Maybe when your spouse said, "Let's go on a picnic with the kids," you replied, "Aw, to hell with it, I don't like picnics," rather than try it. If you aren't re-learning things, when the end of the year and inventory time roll around, you're apt to say, "To hell with the whole damn thing. I've accomplished nothing," and go back to drinking. That one-year point is very critical. Now you've progressed into the two-year point. As my friend the therapist said, "What the hell are you talking about?" What I'm talking about is that you are still in extreme danger of drinking. One important thing that begins to happen (after that one-year high) is that instead of building up highs, the pattern begins to descend toward a low, permanently low, urge to drink. The flare-ups becomes further and further apart, and the intensity of the urge to drink becomes less and less. That's a real landmark.

During that one- to two-year period, your group therapy may be non-directed. By *non-directed* is meant a group which is not led by a trained counselor. If you're an A.A. member, you would start to circulate among A.A. groups to see what they're discussing or what kind of people they are. Don't narrow yourself to one group. Contrary to many people in A.A., I don't recommend anyone doing Step 12 work until a year without drinking has been completed. Many A.A. members (after abstaining for a couple of weeks or months) try to help other people, but I think they are not in a condition to do this. When I've been asked to talk at open A.A. meetings, I've said this. I think some people don't like it, but I sincerely believe it. I think some people return to drinking because they're working with people who don't know what the hell they're talking about. They haven't recovered sufficiently themselves to give advice. If you've worked at re-learning for a year, you're probably in good-enough shape to try to help others. In fact, you should try to help other people as part of your own recovery.

Even at the end of two years you'll get those flare-ups, so still expect a drinking urge. The other day a man told me that after two years without alcohol one evening he began to shake. He was shaking so badly that he couldn't read the newspaper. He didn't know what was happening but soon began to get those old messages: *Get a drink, dummy; get a drink. You're getting shaky.* He hadn't had a drink in two years. What did this mean? It was a flare-up. He didn't know what to do, but he had some Antabuse in the house and fortunately took that instead of the whiskey he also still had in the house. (One of the later talks will cover Antabuse.) Antabuse can be used as an aid, and part of your re-learning is looking for additional help. Antabuse could be one of them because it is very effective in this period.

GOOD (UP TO THREE YEARS)

Now we enter the three-year period. Some people might say that I'm out of my mind talking about three years of recovery, but I didn't make this up. Someone with a similar viewpoint is Dr. Russell Smith of Brighton Hospital, Brighton, Michigan, who is probably the leading authority on alcoholism in the Michigan area. He agrees on the three-year period and has even extended it beyond that. Other people who have worked with alcoholics (including myself) make this same observation. If the condition is good up to the three-year period, most people don't need much training in that second- and third-year period. They do need non-directed therapy, and they need to work on their social life (although by that time they are generally pretty comfortable with it). If they've exposed themselves to them, drinking situations won't bother them at all.

EXCELLENT (UP TO FOUR YEARS)

The flare-ups continue on this downward slide to the four-year point. The continuation of flare-ups is what Dr. Smith is probably talking about when he recommends four years before considering yourself stabilized.

During the third and fourth years you should be working in a group-therapy setting, such as A.A. or any other type of group. You make up your own mind. By this time you'll be a better person socially than you've ever been before—able to cope and compete in any social situation. You'll be the type of man or woman you want to be. All that will be coming across very easily to you. You've been in a 4-year re-learning situation; this shows how badly ingrained people are with the learned behavior of alcoholism.

STABLE (BEYOND FOUR YEARS)

Beyond the four-year period, you stabilize your condition. If you were a cancer patient, we could think of your disease as going into remission. Disease is still there even after four years, although the symptoms are in remission. You're not experiencing the symptoms of your disease, but you still have the disease. In fact, the disease has progressed. If you returned to drinking now, the effect would be as though you've been drinking for four years. It would be devastating. It would be worse than the first time you experienced the symptoms of alcoholism, because the disease progresses. It's difficult to understand, but that's one thing that characterizes alcoholism as a disease. You do not cure the disease by staying away from alcohol; you simply put it into remission. From four years on to what we call the end of your life you should be using a varying therapy, i.e., A.A., hospital therapy groups, and helping other alcoholics, whatever's your preference. You will develop the habit of learning, as opposed to so much re-learning now. Through learning, without alcohol, you expand the complete horizon of your life. Whatever it is you want to do, go ahead and do it. I've seen recovering alcoholics do tremendous things—things that in no way at all could they have done at one point in their lives. They do it with apparent ease; alcoholism is the only major disease with that prognosis. You can become an extremely strong person. Abilities that were latent and underdeveloped before begin to mushroom and sprout. Now something else happens here: the urge to drink leaves. Because of all your hard work, it finally leaves.

IRONY OF DEATH

Some people with faulty thinking can be quite ironic about alcoholism, saying, "Why should I go through all this crap when I'm going to end up dead anyway? Hell, I might as well keep drinking." Well, it isn't me telling you that. Your own mind is. Yes, even if you do something about this drinking you'll end up dead because everybody does. No one's beat that rap yet. It's really ironic, though, how many people make the decision to keep on drinking because they'll die anyway. Unfortunately, their deaths are usually unpleasant, because as I told you before, alcohol doesn't kill by having you go to a party one night, poison yourself with alcohol, and then have a nice, quiet death the next day. It beats the hell out of you—out of your personal integrity, out of your physical body, out of your social interchange with people, out of your job, out of every relationship in your life. It completely shatters you, and then it kills you. You're pretty damn sick when you die, too. There are many people who make that decision to keep on drinking in the face of death, but they're wrong.

TWO THINGS IN RECOVERY

The treatment isn't so bad. Really, it only involves two things:

1. You quit drinking, cross that line into NO MORE ALCOHOL OR OTHER SEDATIVES, not even the little sleeping aid I've mentioned. After six months to one year, you're off any sedation, so certainly after one year you won't need any sedatives for the rest of your life. Under no circumstances should alcohol be used after recovery begins.
2. You CONTINUE THERAPY. A medical doctor (therapist) of Brighton Hospital is an excellent example of continuing therapy. Although he's a leading authority on alcoholism, he attends an A.A. meeting, at least once a week, because he's an alcoholic and realizes the value of therapy. He hasn't had a drink in twenty years, but he is continuing therapy.

Weigh these things in your mind—this concept of time and recovery. Give yourself time. We're talking in terms of four years for the typical alcoholic (man or woman) to become the person he or she wants to be. Although you will continue therapy to the end of your life, your life will be rewarding and fulfilling.

SPIRITUAL FACTORS

The spiritual factors of recovery depend on the individual's outlook on religion to a large extent. The majority of people find that if no apparent solution can be found for a problem in early recovery, relief can be obtained by turning to God (as they know God) for help. Additionally, many alcoholics in the third and fourth year of recovery experience a spiritual awakening when they realize the significance of what they have accomplished. In any event, these spiritual factors are an individual matter, which is beyond the scope of these talks.

RECOVERY CHART

This talk can be extremely useful to the recovering alcoholic if he follows the chart on page 00 and makes a commitment to a four-year recovery program. Individuals should consider all the factors discussed and add additional recovery aids to fit their individual needs. Recovery is still a day-by-day proposition, but at least this plan will give the recovering alcoholic a direction to follow.

The talks which follow are designed to give a few aids to help achieve this goal.

Talk 7

Antabuse

ANTi-Alcohol-aBUSE

If you have disulfiram (Antabuse) in your body and drink alcohol, you will go into physical shock.

Ethyl alcohol
Acetaldehyde   Antabuse blocks
Acetic acid
Carbon dioxide and water

Antabuse is not a cure for alcoholism—it does not remove the urge to drink, just tells you that you will get sick if you drink.

RULES TO TAKE . . .
- you decide
- you take
- you set up contract time
- you tell self, *Why take?*
- you tell somebody before you stop

WHAT IS IT LIKE? . . .
White pills, 250 milligrams usual—can be 125 or 500 milligrams.

CHOICES AFTER TAKING . . .
- take Antabuse—don't drink
- take Antabuse—drink
- don't take Antabuse—drink
- don't take Antabuse—don't drink

PEOPLE CHALLENGE NO POWER OF ANTABUSE

RISKS . . .
- only therapy
- no power challenge

CAN TAKE AS . . .
- daily aid
- emergency aid

Our talk today is on the subject of Antabuse. In our previous talks, we briefly discussed Antabuse as a recovery aid. Today I'd like to continue the subject again because, despite its simple nature, Antabuse can be a deceptive substance to handle.

WHAT IS ANTABUSE?

Antabuse was discovered while searching for a cure for diabetes. In our talk on alcohol damage to the body, we discussed the liver's function of storing glycogen (our food energy) and how glycogen is released into the bloodstream, triggering the pancreas to release insulin, which changes the glycogen into glucose, thereby nourishing us. In looking for a substance which would help the diabetic, whose pancreas produces insufficient amounts of insulin, many oral preparations were tried. One of these was disulfiram. Disulfiram, a chemical substance, didn't solve the diabetes problem, but it did react to alcohol. Disulfiram interferes with the ability of the alcohol in the liver to make a complete chemical transformation. In starting our discussion, we will say first that the word *Antabuse* is a trade name for disulfiram, which is the chemical name. *Antabuse,* in itself, means "anti–alcohol abuse." Let's see how it works.

HOW ANTABUSE WORKS

When we drink alcohol, it is ingested into the body; it enters the stomach, diffuses through the stomach walls, and enters the bloodstream. The blood then courses through the body and enters the liver, where alcohol, being a poison, is broken down. It combines with the enzyme called *alcohol dehydrogenase* and is converted from ethyl alcohol into highly toxic or poisonous acetaldehyde, which is similar to nail polish remover, and then rapidly into acetic acid. We think of acetic acid as

93

vinegar because vinegar is diluted acetic acid. The acetic acid breaks down into carbon dioxide and water, and this is how we expel alcohol from the body. Now if you have Antabuse in your body and drink alcohol, this chemical disulfiram, or Antabuse, prevents the further breakdown in your liver of acetaldehyde into acetic acid. It acts as a chemical block, and you won't convert from acetaldehyde into acetic acid. Consequently, you've poisoned yourself and you become extremely ill. You're liable to be flushed, headachy, weak, and vomiting. Your blood pressure will fluctuate, and your heartbeat will be irregular; you're actually in shock. You become so ill that you'll probably end up in the emergency room of the hospital, where an antidote is given to remove the poisonous acetaldehyde from your body.

HOW IS ANTABUSE USED?

Now you can see how Antabuse can be used to help people with alcohol problems, i.e., if they take Antabuse and drink, they'll become sick. Therefore, they won't drink alcohol. It was thought this would be a cure-all for alcoholism. In fact, a type of therapy called *aversion therapy* is based on this assumption. The idea is to give a person Antabuse, then tell him he can drink all the alcohol he wants. The drinkers aren't told that the Antabuse will make them ill. After repeating this a few times, it was hoped they wouldn't want to drink alcohol. Unfortunately, another problem became quite apparent: Antabuse doesn't remove the desire to drink.

CHOICES TO BE MADE WHILE USING ANTABUSE

If Antabuse is used in recovery, there are still choices to be made, and making them can be difficult. A person might have Antabuse in his system, but there can be no effect from the Antabuse until it's combined with alcohol. Here are the choices:

1. don't drink and continue taking Antabuse;
2. don't drink and don't take Antabuse;

3. don't take Antabuse and return to drinking; or
4. take Antabuse and drink to see if you get sick.

The first two choices, "Don't drink and continue taking Antabuse" and "Don't drink and don't take Antabuse," combined with other therapies may or may not help in recovery from alcoholism. If you don't take Antabuse and drink or if you take Antabuse and drink, you'll get sick. If you're an alcoholic and continue using either of these last two choices, you'll end up dead. There's no question about it. In other words, you are still faced with the responsibility of making decisions.

RISKS WITH ANTABUSE

There are certain risks involved with Antabuse, although people who use it often disregard them. The risks are as follows:

1. You risk challenging the power of Antabuse. You may say, "No pill is telling me I can't drink," and you go ahead and drink. If you think of Antabuse as your master instead of your servant, you may encounter a psychologically deadly problem. If you're the type of person who doesn't like a master, you will fight the Antabuse, and of course the way to do that is to drink.
2. There is a risk if Antabuse is the only recovery tool used. In other words, you may say, "I'm on Antabuse, so I'm all set now." However, you could stop taking Antabuse, and this then becomes the first step in your return to drinking.

ACTUAL USE OF ANTABUSE

How do we use Antabuse? Well, it's generally prescribed by a doctor in 125-, 150-, or 500-milligram tablets which look a little like aspirin. It is taken every day to build to a certain level in the body, and there are very few, if any, side effects. It's prescribed by a doctor because a bad heart or respiratory, blood pressure, or similar problems combined with

95

the reaction of Antabuse and a drink could kill. Some people using Antabuse react to the alcohol in mouthwash, cologne, or shaving lotions. Some people are sensitive and some aren't. If you react to any of these substances, you should either not use Antabuse or ask the doctor to decrease the dosage in order to decrease your reaction.

RULES FOR USE OF ANTABUSE

Another matter of importance is that you take the Antabuse yourself, not have it given to you by another person. You should become responsible for taking it. There are several rules which should be followed when Antabuse is taken:

1. When you take Antabuse each day, you should either verbally or mentally tell yourself why you are taking it. It takes only a few seconds to tell yourself, "I'm taking Antabuse to stop me from drinking because drinking alcohol makes me very ill," or something similar. Don't just take it as a matter of course. During early recovery, you should take it for about six months, although time varies with individual needs.
2. I think that it's very important to make a contract with yourself. If you say you're going to take it for six months, then regardless of what happens (except in an extreme medical emergency), stay on the Antabuse. Then, if you're honest with yourself, you won't go off the Antabuse and start drinking. Make sure that other people know when you're getting off Antabuse so they can help you when your contract is fulfilled. Removal of the protection of Antabuse could lead to drinking.

FEELINGS REGARDING ANTABUSE

Feelings play an important role when you're on Antabuse. Some people have quite negative feelings because they know that Antabuse will cut them off from alcohol, which has been the solution to their problems. This can be terrifying to the person who has used alcohol as a problem solver for a period of time. Some people feel sleepy or a turn-off feeling

96

from using Antabuse, as an example. We can't underestimate this possible negative effect. Not being aware of it could be crucial to continuance in the use of Antabuse.

ANTABUSE A CURE-ALL?

Don't use Antabuse as a panacea (end to all your problems), because Antabuse doesn't affect the desire to drink. A recovery program not involving chemicals is ideal but will not work for all people. Mainly, the reason I'm discussing Antabuse is to caution you not to think of this chemical as a cure-all. It is not. It's a helpful tool, but it is not a cure.

EMERGENCY AID

Antabuse can also be used as a crutch to combat flare-ups as they occur. You may not be on Antabuse every day in the later stages of recovery, but if you notice you're thinking about alcohol and wanting to take a drink, you may find it helpful to have Antabuse in the house. Then you can take a couple of tablets and tell yourself, *Okay, go ahead and drink, because you'll get sick.* This will buy you time in finding help to prevent you from drinking.

POSSIBLE TRAP

To summarize any comments on Antabuse: Used properly, it's an excellent recovery aid. Used improperly, it's a trap, which may lead you back to drinking. Don't rely on Antabuse alone, but use it in conjunction with other recovery aids. Avoid that big trap.

MARKETING OF ANTABUSE

Ayerst Laboratories of New York City, which markets Antabuse, has some excellent literature on the subject, which is generally available through the physician prescribing the drug.

Talk 8

Alcoholics Anonymous and Alternatives

A. A.
ALCOHOLICS ANONYMOUS

- Started 1935, Akron, Ohio
- In 1972 had estimated 250,000 members

Open meeting
Closed meeting   Listings in phone books
Alanon
Alateen

TWELVE STEPS

1. Admit.
2. Higher Power.
3. God's will.
4. Moral inventory.
5. Nature of wrongs.
6. Defects of character.
7. Shortcomings.
8. Amends list.
9. Amends action.
10. Personal inventory.
11. Meditation and prayer.
12. Spread message and help others.

BENEFITS
- Non-drinking peer group
- Friendship
- Simple means to sobriety?
- Group therapy
- Information
- Recovery by example

This talk also covers one of our greatest recovery aids—Alcoholics Anonymous (A.A.)—and alternatives to A.A. My reason for discussing alternatives to A.A. is that, despite the wonderful help A.A. gives people, some people do not like A.A. and I want those people to be aware of other sources of help.

THE FOUNDING OF A.A.

A.A. was founded in Akron, Ohio in 1935 by Bill W. and Dr. Bob. Its basic philosophy is told in the Serenity Prayer:

> God grant me the serenity
> to accept things I cannot change,
> courage to change the things I can,
> and the wisdom to know the difference.

Most A.A. meetings open with that prayer. There are over 1 million members worldwide. It is claimed that fifty percent of their members recover immediately and twenty-five percent after a few slips, with the remainder improving if they stay in A.A. It's hard to prove, so I don't know how true this might be. The average member in A.A. has about two and three quarter years of "no drinking." A.A. is listed in all phone books, so you can always find out where meetings are being held. Meetings are generally held in most metropolitan areas every night of the week, along with some early morning or afternoon meetings.

TRADITIONS OF A.A.

A.A. is based on the following twelve traditions (paraphrased):
1. The common welfare should come first.
2. There is one ultimate authority, a loving God, and the leaders of A.A. are only servants.

3. The only member requirement is a desire to stop drinking.
4. Each group is autonomous and retains its own ability to function.
5. Each group's primary purpose is to get across the alcoholic message.
6. Members can't endorse anything or lend the A.A. name to anything.
7. A.A. is self-supporting and doesn't solicit funds from anybody.
8. It's non-professional.
9. A.A. is purposely not highly structured but has service boards.
10. A.A. is not political.
11. No promotional or advertising use of A.A. is allowed.
12. Its anonymity places its principles above personalities in A.A.

These traditions are difficult for some people, but when you consider them, it seems obvious that the traditions themselves are one of the reasons for the success of A.A.

A.A. STEPS TO RECOVERY (PARAPHRASED)

Certain steps are suggested but not required for A.A. members. These twelve steps are:

1. Admit you are powerless over alcohol. As we discussed in Time and Recovery, that particular step isn't too difficult. Admitting that you are powerless over alcohol doesn't cut you off from alcohol.
2. A higher power can restore sanity. Many people interpret this as having a religious meaning; in other words, the power is God. However, the higher power could be a therapist or another person who can help you because he has a better understanding than you of the problem of alcoholism.
3. Turn life and will to God as we understand Him. That's an important concept. You may reach a point in your life where you can't help yourself and nobody else seems able to help you either. You may then turn to alcohol for help, and that may be fatal if you're an alcoholic. So the type of relief that you're looking for may come from God, and this gives you some escape or "outlet"—someone to help you.
4. Take a moral inventory in order to understand what you're doing and how you're doing it—for example, how you're treating people and how you're treating yourself. Then make corrections as required. Inventory itself is of no use unless you decide to do something about

the things that are wrong in your moral inventory.

5. Admit your wrongs, where possible. Your wrongs should be corrected, but don't dwell on them, particularly around other people. You should think of yourself as Number One in your life and do something about your own problems or wrongs first, before trying to help others.

6. Ask God to remove your character defects. The mention of God affects some people negatively, but again it could also mean a higher power or one's own power is first required to accomplish this task.

7. Have God remove our other shortcomings. Again, God has to be a power as you understand it, and you will have to work at overcoming your own shortcomings.

8. Make a list of all those people you've harmed.

9. Make amends to those people. This doesn't mean you have to list every little thing you did to anybody and then force yourself on them to make amends. The idea is to try to make up for the things you've done wrong, within reason. These tools are all designed to make you feel better about yourself and to get other people to recognize that you're doing something about your problem with alcohol—which in itself should make you feel better about yourself.

10. Continue the personal inventory and correct wrongs at once. Again, this is a continuous recovery program where you will work on your personal inventory and do something about it.

11. Pray for God's help and meditate. Sometimes people make a purely religious interpretation here and depend on God to do their job. Spiritual help is available to those who first help themselves.

12. Carry the message to other alcoholics. It's called 12-stepping. I think the problem here is that people begin 12-stepping when they can't help themselves yet. I wouldn't suggest any 12-stepping until a person has been without alcohol for a year. Until then, he is not in a stable condition, which is necessary to help others.

If you follow the twelve steps of the A.A. program, you can be very successful in your recovery.

A.A. MEETINGS (CLOSED)

Some people have no idea what an A.A. meeting consists of, so I'd like to describe a typical meeting for you. Some of the members will greet you at the door, but they don't make a big scene about it. They tell you where the coffee and refreshments are and may introduce you to a few members prior to the meeting to make you feel comfortable. The people are very congenial and helpful. Once the A.A. meeting begins, the chairman will read the Serenity Prayer and review the traditions and perhaps the twelve steps of A.A. Then they usually break into groups by setting up a table for each of the twelve steps. Sometimes two or three steps are combined at one table, which gives you an opportunity to discuss your problems with other groups. In effect, A.A. is group therapy. One of the problems in A.A. is that sometimes you hear a series of drunka-logues about other people's history, which is not the sole intent of an A.A. meeting. If this is your problem with A.A., try different groups until you find a group of people that you like.

A.A. MEETINGS (OPEN)

Open meetings are also held in which outside members and speakers talk about the problems of alcohol. Family members and interested people can attend the open meetings to learn about the problems of alcohol and to learn about the A.A. program. The meetings are generally pleasant get-togethers, and you receive a great deal of sincere help.

ALANON

Alanon is a branch of A.A. which was organized to assist family members in dealing with their problems. The lives of these non-drinkers are deeply affected by the alcoholic and his problems. In Alanon these family members have an opportunity to air their problems, too.

ALATEEN

Alateen has also been organized to help teenagers deal with alcoholic parents or other family members. It provides a place for them to try to work out their problems and hopefully they will not be as affected or scarred by the alcohol abuse in their family.

ALTERNATIVES TO A.A.

We can see that A.A. is generally a wonderful group for working with alcoholics and problem drinkers. Unfortunately, A.A. is not for everyone. For those who might find it unacceptable, there are alternatives. One of these alternatives is the out-of-hospital oriented programs available in most general hospitals today, where instructional meetings are held in which talks are given. Another possibility is a therapy group. These groups may be directed by alcohol therapists or be self-directed. The individual is exposed to some type of therapy in which he can talk about his problems, listen to the problems of others, and work out a recovery program again in a hospital-sponsored program setting. However, I think that, as they become more comfortable in recovery, many people like to avail themselves of A.A. For example, a recovering alcoholic who travels will feel comfortable visiting with the various A.A. groups and also enjoy their camaraderie. A.A. groups help you feel at home while traveling about the country. In some people's minds, A.A. is the most wonderful resource available for recovering alcoholics. However, if it's not for you, don't tell yourself you can't be helped, because you can. Avail yourself of some of the other groups.

Don't become an A.A. zombie or a person who constantly attends A.A. meetings but does not participate in other forms of recovery. These people are afraid to participate in other areas of social life because of a fear of returning to drink. They are not well rounded in recovery and are generally miserable. They really constitute a misuse of A.A. by punishing themselves due to guilt over their past drinking history. Remember, used correctly, A.A. participation can be a pleasant experience and a valuable aid to recovery.

Additional literature is available on A.A. practices at most A.A. meetings; therefore, I will not dwell on the subject further. Suffice to say the mere presence of A.A. is probably responsible for the recovery aids available to alcoholics today.

Talk 9

Troubled People

Irrational Ideas

- I must be loved by everybody.
- I must be good at everything, or I think I'm a dummy.
- There are bad people in the world who should be punished.
- Things are not going right, so I am in a hell of a mess.
- I'm unhappy but can't do a thing about it.
- I know it's going to happen, and I'm worried sick.
- If I don't do anything about this problem maybe it will go away.
- I can't do anything without help.
- I have a lousy past; therefore I will have a lousy future.
- I must become emotional about other people's problems if I'm to be a good person.
- If I don't solve all my problems it will kill me.

This talk on "troubled people" is designed to cover common attitudes and problems that people share but some people think are unique to them as individuals and use as excuses to continue drinking. Specifically, what we are talking about is a person's attitude toward even reading a book on alcoholism and his attitude toward drinking alcohol. I shall mention a few attitudes briefly, because if you look at some of them you'll find that you're really not unique in your thoughts. You may have thoughts in common with other people, as shown by the following attitudes.

Negative Attitudes

Attitude 1.　Some people might read a book like this and comment, "To hell with it. I'm bored. I'm not interested." In fact, they may even fall asleep, because it's a known psychological reaction that people when exposed to something they don't like often fall asleep.

Attitude 2.　Another common attitude is to follow the crowd. "A lot of people are drinking, and I might as well, too. The whole crowd of people I go around with drink."

Attitude 3.　People may look at this book with a "know-it-all" attitude. "I don't need anything like this. I've heard all those arguments and stories."

Attitude 4.　"The doctor who treats me or the judge is a bigger drunk than I."

Attitude 5.　"I just do what people tell me. I try not to get in a hassle or anything. If they want me to drink, I drink."

Attitude 6.　"You're not showing me anything. I'm tough. I've been through it all."

Attitude 7.　"Help me. I'm helpless, I can't help myself. You help me."

Attitude 8.　Contrary to Attitude 7 is the attitude "I can do it all; I don't need any help." As mentioned previously, recovery from alcohol abuse can rarely be accomplished alone, because we have a habit of "conning" ourselves.

Attitude 9. Some people resent being at a lecture on alcohol abuse, because they believe their alcoholism is a moral problem. Particularly, alcoholics feel it is a moral problem, rather than a disease, and they even resent having to listen to anything about alcoholism.

Attitude 10. "Who wants to be with a bunch of drunks?"

Attitude 11. "I don't have a drinking problem. Other people may, but I don't." This is a real denial because it's made in the face of evidence to the contrary.

Attitude 12. "I'm a social drinker." Have you seen these signs that read: "If you have to drink to be social, that's not social drinking?" People say, "I just want to go someplace, have a good time, be sociable, and use alcohol to loosen up." Well, that's not social drinking—that's pathological or troubled drinking.

Attitude 13. "Poor me, why do I have all these problems? I'm really entitled to a drink to make me feel better."

Attitude 14. "I agree with everything this book says. I really like this, but it doesn't actually apply to me. Just give me a drink, and I'll feel better about everything."

There are many attitudes. We could go on and on. You could, perhaps, list a few attitudes of your own, but I think if you compared notes with other people, you'd find that you're not really different from them.

Really, part of the difficulty we face in the recovery program is the trouble we have with negative attitudes, which are really part of the denial problem. What we should say is, "I recognize that I have a drinking problem, and I want this book to help me help myself in resolving this problem"—a good, honest, open attitude. That's what recovery is about.

IRRATIONAL IDEAS

Other things I would like to mention on the subject of troubled people are the ideas that a well-known psychologist, Albert Ellis, Ph.D., has identified and labeled "irrational ideas."* People have irrational

*Albert Ellis, Ph.D., *A New Guide to Rational Living* (North Hollywood, California: Wilshire Books, 1975), pp. 119–22.

ideas and I'd like to go through some of the ones that are common to many troubled people, including alcohol abusers. An irrational idea is one that really doesn't make sense when examined. Sometimes we begin to think that *our* problems are unique, but they are usually shared by others. The following are a few of these irrational ideas that we form toward common people problems:

1. Some people have the idea that it is a dire necessity for an adult human being to be loved or approved by virtually every person in his or her community. In a nutshell, what they're saying is, "I must be loved by everybody. Otherwise, I'm worthless."
2. Some people have the idea that one should be thoroughly competent, adequate, and achieving in all possible respects if one is to consider oneself worthwhile. This could be: "I must be good at everything, or I am a dummy." Many people strive for excellence in everything. Every time they can't achieve, they feel they're inadequate.
3. Some people have the idea that certain persons are bad, wicked, or villainous and that they should be severely blamed and punished for their villainy. This means that some people think there are bad people in the world who should be punished. They think they're those bad people. Therefore, they should be punished, so they punish themselves, sometimes with alcohol abuse.
4. Some people have the idea that it is awful and catastrophic when things are not the way one would very much like them to be. They say, "Things are not going right, so I'm in a heck of a mess." This applies to all areas of their lives and they're always in a quandary because, for most people, things don't always go right. But we learn to cope with problems that are part of everyday living.
5. Some people have the idea that human unhappiness is externally caused and that people have little or no ability to control their sorrows and disturbances. In other words, they say, "I'm unhappy, but I can't do a thing about it." They throw in the towel, and they think they have no ability to do anything about life. On the contrary, there are many things you can do; if one thing doesn't work, you try something else.
6. Some people have the idea that if something is or may be dangerous or fearsome, one should be terribly concerned about it and should keep dwelling on the possibility of its occurring. In other words, they know it's going to happen and they're worried sick. If they keep it up, they will worry themselves sick. All you can really do is try

to apply a solution to a problem. Instead of being terribly concerned and afraid, try to work out a solution . . . and try that solution. If that doesn't work, then try another solution.

7. Some people have the idea that it is easier to avoid than to face certain life difficulties and self-responsibilities. In other words: "If I don't do anything about this problem, maybe it will go away. I'll just bury my head in the sand." But your problem doesn't go away. Your problem remains the same, gets smaller, or escalates. If you face up to your difficulties and responsibilities, you learn to manage these problems so you can do something about them.

8. Some people have the idea that they should be dependent on others and they should have someone stronger than themselves on whom to rely. That's a common problem. Some people fall into the pit and believe they can't do anything without help, nor will they try. Even with help, you've got to help yourself. Others can't do it all for you. A surprising number of people fall into this trap.

9. Some people have the idea that one's past history is an all-important determiner of one's present behavior and that because something once strongly affected one's life, it will have a similar effect indefinitely. In other words, people say, "I'm still a bum because ten years ago I was drinking and fooling around, not doing things right, and I'll never get over that. I'll always have this mess." That's not true. Thousands of people have proved that isn't true.

10. Some people have the idea that one should become quite upset over other people's problems and disturbances. In other words, they say, "I must become emotionally involved with his or her problems or I'm a no-good bum." And many people carry out that philosophy to a great extent. However, it is more important to introduce the concept of being Number One—in other words, think of yourself first. Do something about what's bothering you and get yourself squared away. Then you can help other people. Some people think this is selfish, but it isn't. How can you possibly help other people unless you help yourself first? You don't have to become involved in everybody's problems. You do as much as you can within the confines of your own abilities.

11. Some people have the idea that there is invariably a right, precise, and perfect solution to human problems and that it is catastrophic if this perfect solution is not found. In other words: "If I don't solve all my problems, it will kill me." And with that attitude, their problems do kill them. It isn't necessary to solve all your problems.

Many people with drinking problems blow their problems out of proportion so they can't handle them. Later on, they find they can. They find they still have the same problems but then can manage them. We don't have to solve all our problems because all problems are not immediately solvable. Many contingent factors are attached to those problems. Mainly, I hope this indicates to you some of the irrational ideas which troubled people have. Much of what I mentioned is taken from the concept of Rational-Emotive Therapy, which is a type of psychological therapy that is quite direct, pointing out the way people think and trying to give direction.

SOLUTION OF PROBLEMS

That their problems are not unsolvable is one of the things which people should be aware of in recovery, whether they're alcoholics, problem drinkers, or neither. Merely getting away from alcohol won't solve these problems. You have to work on them and learn to handle them. Your problems will not go away until you give up drinking, and even then they won't go away. However, you'll be able to manage them. Oftentimes people who drink for many, many years are like adolescents in their personalities and in their ability to manage problems. They don't act in a mature and adult manner, as we mentioned earlier. Once they give up drinking, their ability to solve problems increases and they turn into fairly well-rounded, mature persons.

If you dwell on irrational thoughts, you will justify in your own mind a return to drinking. A.A. calls this *stinking thinking*. Alcohol abusers will continue to develop irrational ideas to allow themselves to abuse alcohol without guilt. Irrational thinking is a big deterrent to recovery that must be monitored continuously during the recovery process. One of the values of group therapy is in having others expose your irrational thoughts to you and help you to think logically and rationally.

During recovery, become aware of the thoughts of mentally healthy people, and compare your thoughts to theirs as a measure of the rationality of your own thinking. If your thinking is troubled and won't improve, you should probably look for some professional help, because a mentally healthy mind is essential to a good recovery program.

Talk 10

Why Continue Drinking?

- **ADDICTION (Need) CANNOT BE CONTROLLED**
- **FEELINGS SCALE**

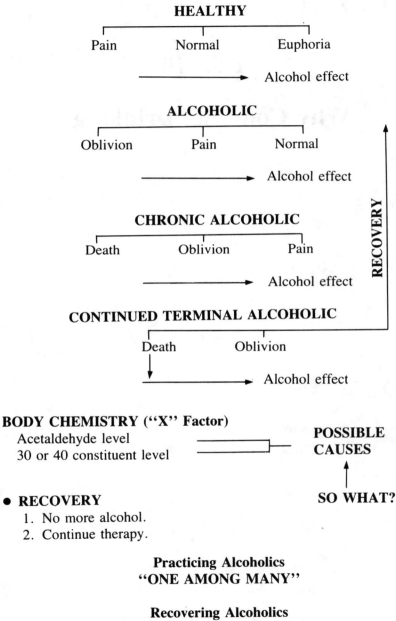

HEALTHY

| Pain | Normal | Euphoria |

⟶ Alcohol effect

ALCOHOLIC

| Oblivion | Pain | Normal |

⟶ Alcohol effect

CHRONIC ALCOHOLIC

| Death | Oblivion | Pain |

⟶ Alcohol effect

CONTINUED TERMINAL ALCOHOLIC

| Death | Oblivion |

⟶ Alcohol effect

RECOVERY

BODY CHEMISTRY ("X" Factor)
Acetaldehyde level
30 or 40 constituent level

**POSSIBLE
CAUSES**

↑

SO WHAT?

- **RECOVERY**
  1. No more alcohol.
  2. Continue therapy.

**Practicing Alcoholics
"ONE AMONG MANY"**

**Recovering Alcoholics
"ONE AMONG FEW"**

Talk 10 covers why people continue drinking. Why do people continue drinking ethyl alcohol when they know it is causing them serious physical and mental problems and all evidence indicates that they are destroying their lives and the lives of other people? These are people who, regardless of wealth or religious belief or background, continue drinking, despite investing much time and effort in treatment.

The reason is addiction, which means "need." Because of real physical addiction, psychological addiction, or a combination of the two, these people need alcohol to get along in life. When I say need, I mean need: as people need food, some people need alcohol. The ability to break the need leads to successful recovery. People with addiction or need have trouble getting along in life without alcohol because a so-called normal life pattern for these people involves the use of alcohol. Life without alcohol becomes abnormal, and these people have extreme difficulty with living.

In a feelings scale, we have normal feelings in the middle, to the right pain, and to the left euphoria. In the beginning, as we add alcohol to the body, we move towards euphoria—feelings of well-being or feelings of being the type of person we want to be. Then a strange thing happens. After a period of time involving alcohol abuse, the scale shifts. Addiction occurs, and what should be normal becomes a center of pain. Now when we drink, we don't move toward a state of euphoria, because that's out of sight, but we experience a temporary euphoria. For most people, this temporary euphoria is a normal state. For the person addicted to alcohol, the normal state most people experience is the best the addict can get with alcohol. If we move the other way from the normal point (for alcoholics), which is a pain level, we move toward oblivion. If we drink over longer periods of time, oblivion becomes the normal way of life for the alcoholic. If he continues drinking, he moves toward the pain level, instead of euphoria. In other words, his normal drinking feelings are pain feelings now. There's no euphoria there. From his normal oblivious state he may move toward death, because the normal feelings that most people experience are far away for the alcoholic. The euphoria that people normally get from drinking alcohol can't be reached. At this

117

point, the person is a chronic alcoholic, generally ready for hospitalization. It is this effort to maintain a degree of normalcy that may cause people to continue drinking.

To correct this tendency toward drinking, these chronic alcoholics must readjust their norm. If they stay away from alcohol, the scale will move back. However, as they get back to an alcoholic normal they'll want to drink again. In other words, their normal will become the pain level, no longer the oblivion level. Once their normal is the pain level, they'll want to drink again to achieve the normal level of non-drinkers. They can't do it. What they have to do is shift the scale and come back to a real normal.

This process called *recovery* involves completely shifting the feelings scale all the way back. Also, you have to begin shifting yourself in relation to this scale. Removing alcohol tips the scale back, but you have to work on a recovery program to shift yourself back. The inability to shift the feelings scale properly is why most people continue to drink. This is somewhat analytical, but another way of looking at this is to apply some good common sense. If you drink over a period of years, you establish normal feelings while in a drunken or intoxicated state and they become your normal way of feeling. An intoxicated state for other people is a normal state for you. If you continue drinking, you'll pass this drunken state, which is a false euphoria, into oblivion. If you continue drinking beyond that, you'll drink yourself to death, as many people do. We talked about some of that in our talk on time and recovery.

Lately, literature on this subject has suggested other theories about why people continue to drink. One of the theories is that body chemistry requires a certain degree of normalcy and that alcoholics have abnormally high acetaldehyde levels. We discussed that in Talks 3 and 7. These abnormally high acetaldehyde levels cause people who are alcoholics not to feel right when that level drops. They're not in a poisoned state, and in order to raise themselves back up to a somewhat poisonous state they drink ethyl alcohol. By drinking alcohol, the acetaldehyde level in their body rises and they feel better. Of course, adjusting acetaldehyde levels by drinking alcohol becomes self-defeating. When monitored on a statistical basis comparing alcoholics with non-alcoholics, a certain body chemistry pattern was noted among alcoholics. Some tests indicated a measure of thirty or forty body chemistry levels or constitutents, such as red blood cells verses white blood cells, the degree of zinc, chrome, or trace elements in the body, clotting factors in the blood, and numerous other factors. Hopefully some work will continue in this area and we may be able to detect alcoholics before the symptoms are triggered with alcohol or determine whether alcoholism is due to periodic abuse or long-term abuse of alcohol. The unknown X factor in alcoholism may be defined someday.

There are many failures in recovery because people continue drinking in the face of mounting evidence that this is self-destructive. Unfortunately, there are more failures than successes. It is hoped that these talks will help a few more people to successfully arrest an alcohol abuse problem.

The successes that I have seen are generally outstanding if a person is willing to stay away from alcohol for about four years and work at re-learning life without alcohol as outlined in these talks.

Some of the so-called rapid recoveries from alcoholism by celebrities as announced in the media are not true due to the absence of sufficient time to achieve a stabilized recovery. Many times you will later hear that these people have gone back to alcohol. Those who are successful have been working at recovery for a significant number of years, not just a few weeks in a detox center. Don't be deceived by misinformation.

Talk 11

Alcohol-related Hypoglycemia

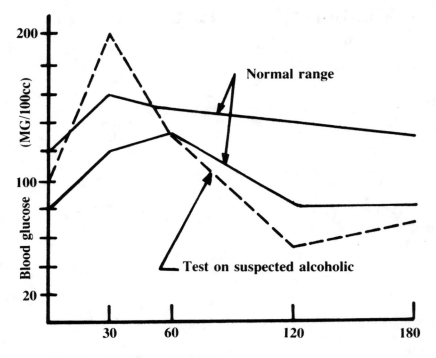

Results of Glucose Tolerance Test
Reactive Hypoglycemia in Alcoholism

Normal range

Test on suspected alcoholic

(MG/100cc)

Blood glucose

200

100

20

30   60   120   180

Minutes after ingesting glucose

One of the problems confronting the alcoholic is the possible development of a medical disorder called hypoglycemia. A discussion on hypoglycemia, in layman's terms, as it pertains to alcoholics is the subject of our talk today.

WHAT IS HYPOGLYCEMIA?

In the simplest terms, hypoglycemia can be called low blood sugar, which is the opposite of hyperglycemia, known as diabetes or high blood sugar.

Our body cells are nourished primarily by a combination of sugar (in the form of glucose) and oxygen, both of which are carried to the body cells by the blood system. If the blood sugar level is abnormally low or fluctuates rapidly or widely, the body cells, in particular the sensitive brain cells, are improperly nourished and the brain will not function properly, which can lead to erratic behavior and other symptoms.

Some medical people believe that hypoglycemia, in its various forms, may be the cause of alcoholism or may be the factor that causes destructive drinking in the alcoholic. There is, apparently, some connection between alcoholism and hypoglycemia. However, it has never been conclusively proven that all hypoglycemics are alcoholics or vice versa.

WHAT CAUSES HYPOGLYCEMIA?

A simplified explanation of hypoglycemia would begin with a brief explanation of how the body handles food.

The food we eat drops down into the stomach, where it is mixed and broken down by body acids and enzymes. A portion of the food matter is converted into a form of sugar called *glucose*, and in this form it diffuses through the stomach walls and enters the bloodstream. Depending on the complexity of the food, much of this blood-glucose activity continues as the mixed food passes into the intestinal tract.

If the food consumed is liquid sugar, as in some drinks, the food almost immediately appears in the bloodstream as glucose, because very little stomach or intestinal activity is required by the body during the conversion process. If the food is a more complex form of a refined carbohydrate, such as white flour used in bread, the conversion into glucose takes a little longer. And if a more complex carbohydrate, such as fruit, is eaten, a still longer conversion time is required. Eating more complex foods such as proteins, including meat, eggs, fish, nuts, et cetera, leads into even longer time intervals for the conversion into glucose.

After the food enters the bloodstream in the form of glucose, it nourishes our body cells and the excess is stored in the liver in the form of glycogen. After the liver is filled with glycogen, the excess glucose is stored in the body as fat. When the digestive process is complete, the amount of glucose supplied by the intestine to the bloodstream is reduced and the liver will release glycogen, which causes the pancreas to secrete a hormone called insulin, which converts the glycogen back to glucose; we are now being supplied energy by the liver. When our liver glycogen level is depleted, we draw upon the sugar stored as fat in our bodies and convert this fat to glucose in a similar process. This is a complicated body regulatory process, and a healthy body becomes very adept at maintaining a blood sugar level of about 80 to 120 mg. of glucose for each 100 cc of blood, while drawing upon intestinal, liver, and fat glucose supplies. In some people, this process gets out of whack and trouble occurs.

For instance, the diabetic, among other things, can't convert glycogen into glucose effectively because of poor insulin production. Consequently, the body reacts negatively and loses its ability to turn excess glucose into glycogen, leading to large glucose buildups or high blood sugar average levels in excess of 200 mg. per 100 cc of blood, which (without going into detail) results in a myriad of physical problems.

However, the body can also convert glycogen too effectively into glucose because the pancreas consistently produces too much insulin. This leads to a condition called *hyperinsulinism,* which rapidly decreases the glycogen level and subsequently the glucose level in the blood, leading to low blood sugar or hypoglycemia.

Therefore, we can say that hypoglycemia is caused by faulty insulin regulation in the body. This defect can be of a consistent nature, as in functional hypoglycemia, or intermittent, as in reactive hypoglycemia.

ALCOHOL AND HYPOGLYCEMIA

Apparently, when we drink alcohol, this substance rapidly enters our bloodstream, primarily through the wall of the small intestine, and we feel an immediate effect, mainly in the brain. However, ethyl alcohol is a poison which must be broken down in the body. The liver serves this function by having the liver cells break the alcohol into acetaldehyde, then acetic acid, then carbon dioxide and water. In order to perform this function, the liver cells release stored glycogen as they mobilize to attack the poisonous alcohol. The release of liver-stored glycogen, of course, triggers the pancreas to secrete insulin, converting the glycogen to glucose. However, this is an abnormal situation, since the body is entering into this complex metabolic process not on the basis of food energy needs, but because it's being poisoned with alcohol. Eventually, after repeated episodes of triggering this insulin response with alcohol, the delicate system may go awry. Overproduction of insulin may eventually result through a reaction to any type of simple or refined carbohydrate, because their relatively fast rate of absorption into the blood stream mimics alcohol. Apparently, alcohol abusers can become susceptible to this reactive overproduction of insulin.

The problems resulting from hyperinsulinism or low blood sugar can be quickly negated by two different methods: (1) by eating refined carbohydrates, the glucose level of the blood is raised by absorption from the intestinal tract, and (2) by drinking progressive and repeated quantities of alcohol, the liver can be forced to release more glycogen, thereby giving the excess insulin something to convert to glucose. It is postulated that the bodies of certain people, in particular alcoholics, soon become aware of the fact that blood sugar levels can be manipulated by alcohol, and these people consistently abuse alcohol because, unknowingly, they are attempting to restore their blood sugar levels to normal with alcohol.

In any event, in a large number of individuals continued alcohol abuse, particularly when combined with an over-indulgence in refined carbohydrates, can lead to the development of reactive hypoglycemia.

SYMPTOMS OF HYPOGLYCEMIA

The general symptoms of reactive, or alcohol-sensitive hypoglycemia usually occur after consumption of alcohol or ingestion of refined carbohydrates. These symptoms can be the following:
- General nervousness and mental disorientation, which may come close to a psychotic break, so-called nervous breakdown, in severity
- Feeling of weakness physically, particularly in the limbs
- Quick temper and low people tolerance level
- Craving for sugar or alcohol, for apparently unknown reasons
- Temporary relief of symptoms by using sugar or alcohol
- Uncontrollable anxiety
- Headaches and vague body aches
- Flu-like symptoms, without a fever
- Depression and suicidal tendencies or behavior

Usually, the symptoms are not sufficient in intensity to incapacitate people, but they certainly make everyday life exceedingly difficult.

If persons suffering from reactive hypoglycemia go on a refined carbohydrate or alcohol bender, they may require hospitalization to stabilize their metabolism.

DIAGNOSIS OF HYPOGLYCEMIA

Unfortunately, the medical profession, in general, is unsympathetic toward people with hypoglycemia, which makes the availability of diagnosis difficult. However, many doctors are becoming increasingly aware of people with hypoglycemic symptoms and have developed various diagnostic aids. The principal means of diagnosis is the six-hour glucose tolerance test.

There are variations of the glucose tolerance test, but essentially, the test consists of a twelve-hour fast, followed by a test for fasting blood sugar level determined by a blood sample, ingestion of about one hundred grams of glucose in a flavored drink, and then periodic blood samples to determine the blood sugar level at about thirty-minute to one-hour intervals for up to six hours, when testing for hypoglycemia. The effect of the test on the person's feelings, both psychological and physiological, is also sometimes recorded.

The figure on page 129 shows the results of such a test on a person known to have the symptoms of reactive hypoglycemia and also suspected to be an alcoholic. The solid lines in the figure represent the highest values and lowest values—hence the range in values expected from a person in normal, good health, not experiencing either diabetic or hypoglycemic symptoms. The dotted line shows the results of a test on a suspected alcoholic. Note that the fasting blood sugar is normal (100), but that it rises to 200 after thirty minutes (possibly indicating a lag in storing the excess glucose in the liver as glycogen), followed by a rapid decline below normal in one hour, and abnormally low in two hours, which then persists for three hours. This test was terminated at the end of three hours because it appeared that the patient's reaction was subsiding and that the sugar level was returning to the fasting level. The patient reported developing the symptoms of reactive hypoglycemia during the period of 60 to 180 minutes, and he felt an overwhelming compulsion to eat something (preferably sugar) or drink alcohol at the 120-minute mark when the blood sugar level was down to 50. It is thought that the rapid decline from 200 to 50 in 90 minutes is a clear indication of hypoglycemic reaction. Therefore, this person was diagnosed as suffering from hypoglycemia, although no diagnosis for alcoholism was made.

TREATMENT OF HYPOGLYCEMIA

In theory, the treatment of reactive hypoglycemia is relatively simple. For acute attacks, the hypoglycemic is placed on a strict, all-protein diet, i.e., meat, fish, eggs, cheese, et cetera, to be eaten in small quantities every three hours for about seven days. Once the condition stabilizes, only foods relatively low in refined carbohydrates should be eaten, and certainly no sugar, pure carbohydrates, or alcohol should be consumed. Unfortunately, very few people stick to this regimen and repeated relapses occur, which trigger the adverse symptoms of this affliction, resulting in much discomfort to the hypoglycemic, who in many cases turns to alcohol for relief.

Invariably, hypoglycemics attempt to relieve their symptoms with sugar or alcohol because of the fast relief these substances give. However, this can only be self-defeating.

THE ALCOHOLIC-HYPOGLYCEMIC

Because of the uncertainty of their ailment, many people with hypoglycemia are treated for alcoholism. A distinct possibility exists that some people have the disease alcoholism and also the functional disorder of hypoglycemia. These people are in a real quandary, because very rarely will they be treated for each affliction at the same time. They may be admitted to a hospital for alcoholism, and while being detoxed they will be fed large quantities of carbohydrates, including sugar, to restore their liver. This only adds to their discomfort and may actually cause them to return to drinking. On the other hand, if treated as hypoglycemics, they may be encouraged to drink alcohol as a tranquillizer and sedative to slow their metabolism, contributing to both further alcohol difficulties and faulty blood sugar levels.

Unwittingly, the medical profession usually causes these people prolonged grief and physical suffering, which can lead to death by suicide or little hope for recovery from alcoholism.

However, there exist certain alcoholism treatment facilities which recognize the possible involvement of hypoglycemia in an alcoholic's problems or the fact that a person, while not an alcoholic, may react unfavorably to the withdrawal of alcohol. These facilities usually tend to place recovering alcoholics on high-protein, low-carbohydrate diets until the existence or non-existence of hypoglycemia is established.

For those patients suspected not to be alcoholics but to be hypoglycemics, total abstinence from alcohol should be recommended. For those with combined alcoholism and hypoglycemia, total abstinence from alcohol must be recommended. However, a gradual return to the use of refined carbohydrates may be possible after a period of time, but caution with carbohydrates is indicated.

In conclusion, hypoglycemia of a reactive type is a distinct possibility in all cases of alcoholism and probably all alcoholics should be tested for refined carbohydrate intolerance and advised accordingly. Additionally, a great deal of literature is available on the subject, which can be a further aid in controlling this condition.

Talk 12

The Medical Model

As a means of summarizing our previous talks I would like to talk about the medical model of the alcoholic and the general severity of this disease.

ALCOHOLISM AS A DISEASE

Much has been written and said about the disease alcoholism. However, most people still think of this affliction as a moral or social problem.

A few years ago, I gave a talk to a women's group in Westland, Michigan. The talk went well until I began comparing alcohol and diabetes as diseases. At that point a member of the audience who had diabetes and who had a young son with diabetes became highly indignant with the thought that alcoholism could even be considered a disease. This woman steadfastly maintained and was quite loud and vocal that alcoholics are moral lepers who in no way had a disease and in no way should be treated as patients in a hospital. I was shocked but at the same time sympathetic to her attack on what I was saying and it re-emphasized to me that this woman typifies the thinking of most of the public about alcoholism as a disease.

What is alcoholism therapy doing in a hospital? Well, maybe it's there because alcoholism is a disease which, contrary to the beliefs of some people, requires the services of an acute-care hospital in its treatment.

THE DISEASE ALCOHOLISM

As previously discussed in our talks, if we were to take a sample of ten adult Americans and examine their ethyl alcohol drinking habits, we would find the following:

- Two people out of the ten do not use alcohol. This is for several reasons. If you are a Southern Baptist, Moslem, Mormon, Black Mus-

133

lim, or member of one of several other religions, you would not drink alcohol because of your religious beliefs. This religious influence on the use of alcohol can be seen in the strict laws against alcohol abuse in Moslem Saudi Arabia or even in this country by the laws of the heavily Mormon states Utah and Idaho. Additionally, some people don't like the effect of alcohol. They don't like the feelings, both physical and mental, that they get when they drink alcohol. And since we drink the drug alcohol for its effect, if you don't like the effect, you don't drink it and probably discourage others in the abuse of alcohol, including your children.

- Three people out of ten are social drinkers. Now most drinkers claim to be social drinkers. The NIAAA (National Institute of Alcohol Abuse and Alcoholism) used to have a series of billboards in the Detroit area which read:

IF YOU DRINK TO BE SOCIAL,
THAT IS NOT SOCIAL DRINKING

If you question those who claim to be social drinkers, a typical response is: "I drink to enjoy myself at parties, because alcohol loosens me up so I can talk and socialize with people. In fact, the more I drink the more social I become." That's pathological, not social, drinking. This person is drinking to remove some type of personality defect which inhibits his enjoyment of parties without first drugging himself.

When talking to a group of people involved in an alcoholism awareness program because of drinking while driving or people referred to a hospital for in-patient treatments required because of alcohol abuse, you are not talking to social drinkers. You don't see social drinkers in these settings unless they are guests at a particular meeting. These people are probably problem drinkers or alcoholics, although most claim to be social drinkers.

A measure of social drinking is the fact that social drinkers very rarely let their blood alcohol content exceed .05 percent. In terms of twelve ounce cans of beer, this is about three cans of beer over a three-hour period. If you drink faster than that or more than that, you're not a social drinker. We can see that social drinkers and non-drinkers comprise five out of ten of our sample of ten people or fifty percent of the adult population in this country.

- Four people out of ten are problem drinkers; they consistently drink to blood alcohol levels in excess of .15 percent. That's about nine cans of beer in three hours. At that level, the problem drinker is ready to go to the party and continues to drink to greatly elevated blood alcohol levels. So we can say that problem drinkers reach the good feeling or "mellow glow" at .15 percent. Of course, this becomes a problem, if only for the fact that in forty-eight out of fifty states, a blood alcohol content exceeding .10 percent in a person driving a motor vehicle constitutes drunk driving. Of course, the severity of problem drinking varies from a minor problem to a severe problem.
- One person out of ten adult Americans is a statistical oddball when drinking habits are analyzed. This person is the alcoholic, so named because he suffers from the disease alcoholism. Unfortunately, most alcoholics cannot accept the fact that they have a disease, and since alcoholism, if not arrested, is a terminal disease, the disease kills them.

Based on our statistical sampling of drinking habits, it appears that there exist three broad classifications of drinkers:

Social drinkers
Problem drinkers
Alcoholics

SOCIAL DRINKERS are generally unconcerned and cannot relate to other people's drinking problems. They say typical things like: "I can't understand how someone can get sick on alcohol and yet continue drinking. Why don't they just quit all that lousy drinking?"

PROBLEM DRINKERS, unlike social drinkers, gradually develop a psychological dependence or need for alcohol, which constitutes addiction. They begin to use alcohol casually and eventually learn to use it as a chemical solution to their problems. Of course, this psychological learning process involving alcohol is very difficult to unlearn, and therefore problem drinkers begin to exhibit all kinds of behavior problems associated with their drinking. This, of course, leads to deteriorating physical and mental health in many cases, because ethyl alcohol is a poison. However, since their problem is primarily psychological, most problem drinkers are never sufficiently motivated to change their behavior and do something about their drinking.

ALCOHOLICS also generally develop a psychological dependence, i.e., addiction to alcohol. However, unlike the problem drinker, the alcoholic also develops a true physical addiction to alcohol. It's this physical addiction that, if not arrested, or broken, will eventually cause the death of the alcoholic. Fortunately, it's the physical addiction which eventually seems to motivate the alcoholics to seek help, and due to the physical nature of this disease, it is most essential that this help be available in an acute-care hospital, especially in the early treatment phases.

HOW DOES THE DISEASE DEVELOP?

We can best describe the development of the disease alcoholism by looking at a composite patient history.

Drinking Years

The typical alcoholic begins drinking during the teenage years, and finds that alcohol does some marvelous things. If you're inhibited in social situations, alcohol becomes a great social lubricant which removes these inhibitions. Alcohol also seems to ease the mental stress caused by job, money, religion, sex, domestic, cultural and physical problems, and practically any other problem. The alcoholic soon learns, during the drinking years, that alcohol is a great chemical solution to life's problems, and he gradually develops a psychological addiction to alcohol. Drinking experiences are rewarding and successful because the alcoholic learns to drink and handle life with alcohol during these wonderful drinking years. Unknowingly, a strong and tenacious, extremely difficult-to-break psychological addiction to alcohol is also developed during the drinking years.

Terminal Years

Eventually, the alcoholic crosses an imaginary time line into true alcoholism by triggering the symptoms of the disease which have been latent or dormant. This is an important point because, similar to those people who develop adult onset diabetes, the alcoholic is apparently born with a predisposition to alcoholism and typically begins to exhibit physical symptoms of the disease during the adult years. Once the physical symptoms are apparent, the alcoholic has entered into the terminal stage of the disease and the prognosis is death, unless the disease is arrested. In the terminal state, death is generally not swift but occurs after shortening the alcoholic's natural life span by ten to twenty years. Also, death does not occur by the "have a party, live fast, die young" philosophy, but generally, after the alcoholic is physically and mentally wrecked, when not much remains, death occurs.

Unfortunately, most alcoholics spend their terminal years drinking, having continuing problems, and desperately trying to get back to those "good drinking experiences" which occurred during the drinking years. This is impossible—many people have tried to get back there by many means, but it cannot be done because once the symptoms are triggered, the only recourse is a drinking death or recovery without alcohol.

The terminal nature of the disease cannot be discounted. Of these alcoholics that attempt recovery without alcohol, only about three percent are successful; the other ninety-seven percent succumb to the disease. These figures are based on personal observations of various alcohol rehabilitation programs, ranging from hospitals to A.A. Despite the public claims of various groups regarding recovery programs, much has to be done to reduce the exceedingly high death rate associated with this disease. Alcohol abuse and alcoholism would not be the third leading cause of death, behind heart disease and cancer, in this country if the recovery programs were as successful as some people claim. Let's face the facts. Alcoholism is a terminal killer disease, not a moral or behavioral problem.

SYMPTOMS OF ALCOHOLISM

There are several major symptoms of alcoholism:

- **Increase in tolerance** becomes apparent as a person gradually requires increasingly larger amounts of alcohol to achieve the same effect. Most alcoholics have a large tolerance for alcohol in their early drinking years and are the type of people who drink others under the table.

Alcoholics in the middle stages of the disease can physically handle (or metabolize) large quantities of alcohol.

- **Decrease in tolerance** occurs during the latter disease stage, when apparently the alcoholic's body can no longer handle large quantities of alcohol and the ability to drink declines.
- **Blackouts** indicate the inability of the alcoholic to remember a drinking experience when he is sober. Blackouts are experienced by ninety percent of alcoholics, but not all. These blackouts can include a period of time covering a few minutes to many months. The brain memory cells storing information are apparently lost during the drinking episode. Therefore, the information cannot be retrieved. There are several explanations for blackouts based on body chemistry. Also, the fact that the triglycerides or fat globules released in the bloodstream during the ingestion of alcohol plug the brain capillaries, destroying brain cells, may be an explanation.
- **Long hangovers** which persist for more than twelve hours are an early indication of alcoholism. Certainly, if a hangover lasts more than twenty-four hours, regardless of the quantity of alcohol consumed, this indicates alcoholism. If the disease alcoholism is not present, the body should recover from a drinking bout and the body chemistry stabilize in twenty-four hours. This twenty-four hour limit is also true for alcoholics who have not triggered this symptom of their disease. Alcoholics, in the early stages of the disease, recover from hangovers quite rapidly, thus adding to the deception about their alcoholism.
- **Withdrawal symptoms** differ from the ordinary hangover symptoms, like headache, gastritis, nausea, and general weariness. Withdrawal symptoms generally involve the central nervous system. These include hand or head shaking and tremors, mental disorientation, irregular heartbeat and blood pressure, acute anxiety and depression, fear, and possibly a feeling of impending doom. If withdrawal symptoms are relieved by drinking more alcohol, then the person is definitely an alcoholic. The withdrawal symptoms can be so severe that they may result in a central nervous system collapse and death—which is why many alcoholics are hospitalized and treated for their life-threatening symptoms during withdrawal.

CAUSES OF THE DISEASE ALCOHOLISM

Much has been written about the general cause of alcoholism, and a great deal of research has been done and is continuing to be done on the cause of the disease. Without exploring all factors which may cause alcoholism, we can look at a couple of things which indicate the disease has something to do with inherited and/or developed body chemistry.

Ethyl alcohol, when ingested, enters the bloodstream and is broken down in the body as follows:

> Alcohol to
> Acetaldehyde to
> Acetic acid to
> Carbon dioxide plus water

We can see that alcohol changes into acetaldehyde, which is an extremely poisonous substance, similar to nail polish remover, then into acetic acid (vinegar is dilute acetic acid), and then into carbon dioxide (that fizzy stuff in soda pop) plus water, in which form we eliminate it from the body.

The chemical transformation to acetaldehyde (due to its poisonous nature) can make most people ill. Therefore, the further conversion into acetic acid occurs quite rapidly, as the body's means of preventing general sickness while drinking alcohol. It has been found that alcoholics, as a group, possess an abnormally high level of acetaldehyde when they are not drinking, as compared with the norm of the population. Apparently, alcoholics go around in a slightly poisonous state chemically, due to this acetaldehyde level, and learn to adapt physically and psychologically to the feelings associated with this state. If, for some reason, the alcoholic's acetaldehyde level should drop to so-called normal levels, the alcoholic doesn't feel right and soon learns to correct these feelings chemically by drinking alcohol, which changes into acetaldehyde and restores his feelings.

Another body chemistry study indicated that by measuring the percentage levels of about thirty-five different substances in the blood, such as potassium, sodium, calcium, vitamins, hormones, et cetera, a profile could be drawn that would indicate that if a person's blood chemistry fell within a certain composition range for each of these substances, the person was probably an alcoholic. A blind test, in which researchers were given the blood of alcoholics and non-alcoholics, indicated that they were able to identify the alcoholics in the groups eighty-five percent of the time, based only on a blood chemistry analysis. Apparently, this test is costly, sensitive, and delicate and currently cannot be adapted to use on the general population on a routine basis.

It may soon become possible to identify alcoholics, including non-drinking alcoholics, by some type of body chemistry analysis, and thus we will be able to forewarn people of the presence of this disease in their bodies prior to the development of severe symptoms.

However, knowing the cause of a disease does not necessarily mean that, told the cause, all people with the disease will be able to manage their condition. If we take adult onset diabetes as an example, we find that prior to 1929, when the function of the hormone insulin in the body was discovered, to be diagnosed as a diabetic meant you were terminal and would not live out a normal life span. In fact, years ago, if you had diabetes you were treated like a moral leper, similar to the treatment received by most alcoholics even today. Once insulin was discovered, the medical management of diabetes became available, although no cure exists. Given a specific medical regimen involving diet and drugs, most diabetics now possess the means to control their disease and lead a somewhat normal life. In spite of this, most diabetics will not stick to a rigid medical regimen, don't eat properly or take their medication properly, deny their illness, and repeatedly have relapses into a symptomatic life-threatening disease state.

Alcoholics, even if they know the specific cause of their disease, alcoholism, would in most cases probably not be able to manage to control their disease. They will suffer repeated relapses and, generally, live a life of poor disease control. This is one reason why A.A. has generally maintained that the cause of alcoholism is not the important issue, but rather the management of the disease is what is important. Alcoholics, according to A.A., shouldn't dwell on ''why me?'' but should work on acceptance and control of their disease state.

Therefore, the cause of alcoholism is, in reality, not that important to the suffering alcoholic, and the emphasis should be on disease management or recovery.

AVAILABLE TREATMENT PROGRAMS

Prior to the founding of A.A. in Akron, Ohio, in the mid-1930s, there were only sporadic groups available to help the alcoholic. Since that time, A.A. has grown and the A.M.A. (American Medical Association) and various hospital groups have recognized alcoholism as a medically treatable disease.

Most major hospitals across the United States now offer some form of alcoholism therapy and medical assistance to the alcoholic. The type of therapy and medical service varies widely, since no standardized treatment procedure has evolved to date. As an example of hospital involvement, Henry Ford Hospital, which is the largest hospital in the Detroit metropolitan area, finally set up a separate department to treat alcoholism in 1977. And in 1981 it opened a beautiful fifty-bed complex, funded by industry, solely for the treatment of alcoholism. It is to the credit of this major hospital, which prides itself as a medical clinic second to none, that it has established an alcoholic clinic. On the other hand, many smaller acute-care hospitals, including Annapolis Hospital, Wayne, Michigan, which started an alcoholism program in the mid-1960s, have offered treatment to alcoholics for many years. The hospital programs are also designed to help the problem drinker cope with psychological addiction to alcohol. Social workers at those hospitals not having alcoholism programs will generally refer people to hospitals with the necessary facilities and structure to treat alcoholics. All these hospital programs are gradually improving, and the medical management of alcoholism has become an increasing specialty among medical people. Nowadays there is no excuse for the alcoholic not to turn to a hospital for help.

A.A. (Alcoholics Anonymous) still remains the alcoholic's greatest resource, and most medical programs usually prepare alcoholics for A.A. participation in the management of their disease. Unfortunately, there are some older hardline A.A. people who cannot accept the medical management of their disease, because the medical community spurned alcoholics for so many years. Modern and newer A.A. members, many who have been exposed to medical programs, can appreciate and see the necessary interaction between medical help for the alcoholic combined with A.A. or other therapeutic involvement. Indeed, A.A. offers one of the best organized and dedicated after-care arrangements available for the recovery from a major disease, alcoholism, and compares with organizations dedicated to other diseases such as arthritis, diabetes, multiple sclerosis, et cetera. A.A. does this with very little publicity and no political involvement, according to their creed. The alcoholic is indeed fortunate to have this great A.A. organization available as an aid to recovery.

RECOVERY

Recovery generally is never fully explained to the alcoholic. A talk on time and recovery should present a chronological approach to alcoholism recovery and the aids required in recovery.

Basically, we are talking about a four-year program before an alcoholic is able to effectively manage alcoholism. This program includes these supports:

Medical - nutritional
Medical - physical
Medical - psychological
Psychological support
Directed group therapy (could be A.A.)
Non-directed group therapy (could be A.A.)
Spiritual
Social
Education
Re-learning process
Medical - pharmaceutical
Physical and mental exercise

The alcoholic must learn to recognize and control flare-ups, dry drunks, and a need for alcohol and identify and control the symptoms of the disease.

Above all, the alcoholic must learn to handle life's problems without alcohol as a crutch.

After many years of terminal drinking, our medical model of the alcoholic cannot expect to manage the disease after only one or two days or even weeks or months of recovery. Recovery is a lifelong process, and it is only after about four years of this recovery process that good management of the disease is possible. It is this unawareness of the time required in recovery that leads most alcoholics into relapse. They become either despondent or overconfident about their progress and return to drinking. Also, most alcoholics will not work at recovery; in particular, they will not learn how to do things in life without alcohol.

Recovery from alcoholism consists of simply two factors:

1.   No more alcohol or other sedative drugs
2.   Continuing therapy (possible as a lifelong A.A. member)

Although simple in concept, the recovery from alcoholism is fraught with disaster, and only about 3 percent of alcoholics who start a recovery program are successful, again despite what some groups claim.

From the medical standpoint, alcoholism is probably the only major disease where the prognosis for recovery indicates that the patient, although still possessing a progressive disease, can put the disease in remission and be stronger physically and psychologically than when treatment began.

The fact that alcoholism is a progressive disease, which continues in the absence of the catalyst alcohol, must be clearly understood by the alcoholic. You do not buy time that can be later used for drinking by engaging in a recovery program. The return to alcohol after many years of recovery without alcohol is devastating to the alcoholic, due to the progressive nature of the disease.

Recovery is a slow, lifelong proposition which has its rewards in the apparent betterment on a daily basis of the physical and psychological well-being of the recovering alcoholic.

THE FUTURE

Despite the negative aspects of some of this talk, the future for those alcoholics successful in recovery can be outstanding.

Alcoholics with a long time in recovery are generally exceptional people. They are well rounded in personality, cordial in social conduct, neat in personal habits and appearance, outstanding in a job sense, and confident, solid people. They are generally everything they want to be and more. Their accomplishments exceed their expectations, and the future holds many rewards for them as they maintain a life without alcohol. With a mind and body free from alcohol addiction, their latent energies and potential can be utilized to the fullest extent of their abilities. They learn how to handle life's situations without being drugged, no longer suffer the stigma of their disease, and have an acceptance and serenity that in many cases defies description.

To those alcoholics successful in recovery I can only extend my admiration and awe of the magnificent battle which they have raised against a most insidious, debilitating disease. They hold a light to the future for all people suffering from the disease alcoholism and represent what the future can hold for the medical model of the alcoholic.